It's All About
JESUS
WHAT THEY NEVER TOLD YOU
IN CHURCH

D. R. SILVA

It's All About Jesus: What They Never Told You in Church

ISBN: 978-0615876115
Copyright © 2013, by D. R. Silva

Published by ReKnowMe Pub.
This title is also available for Kindle. Visit www.reknow.me for more info.

Scripture quotes that use italic formatting or ellipses ("...") are done so only for emphasis and do not change or imply change of the original text; neither is it done with the intent to hide anything from the reader. You are highly encouraged to look up every Bible verse used in this book, and read them for yourself in their entire context.

Version 1: (August 2013)

Endorsements

"If only more authors wrote with this kind of honesty, transparency and passion. I believe this book will deeply echo the questions and thoughts of many believers around the world who are tired of the mundane status quo. I highly recommend you read this book slowly and with a highlighter. You'll need a highlighter, trust me."

— **Cornel Marais**, Author and Founder of *CharismaMinistries.org*

"One of the best books on Righteousness, Grace and the New Covenant that I have ever read. Daniel paints a crystal clear picture of why we can stand before God unashamed, totally innocent, unafraid of any punishment and optimistically aware of how God really feels about us. A true gem - I highly recommend it!"

— **Andre van der Merwe**, Author of *Grace, the Forbidden Gospel*

"This book is guaranteed to change the face of Christianity."

— **Ryan J. Rhoades**, Author of *RevivalOrRiots.org*

Author's Note

I don't intend to present the ideas in this book as absolute facts that you must adhere to or suffer divine consequence. I consider the ideas and insights in this book to be merely a matter of personal perspective based on years of experience, observation and participation.

You're not required to believe all of what is said in this book and apply it to your life. You're welcomed to believe some of it; you're welcomed to believe none of it.

As I tell all the fans and supporters of my writing: *test everything and hold on to what is good* (2 Thess. 5:21).

I cannot emphasize that enough.

My goal is to present ideas and perspectives that have helped me live a happier and more complete life.

As the title of this book suggests, I'm sharing ideas and perspectives that you might not otherwise hear about in a typical church service.

I'm forever a student of Life—I ask a lot of questions and I share the answers.

All I'm attempting to offer is a genuine, heartfelt and honest perspective that has brought me Life in Christianity.

You have the choice of whether or not you want to receive what I'm trying to give.

As always, thank you for taking time to read my writing.

D. R. Silva

Acknowledgements

I'd like to acknowledge and thank those who have offered me new perspectives and taught me how to voice the questions and opinions I had kept suppressed and hidden for much of my Christian life.

Shandy – Had you never given me a proper perspective of the finished work of Jesus, neither this book nor my website would exist, and there are many people who wouldn't have been inspired to hope and freedom by my words. I don't want to imagine where I would be had you not taken the risk of offending me.

Ryan – It has been one of my greatest honors to stand next to you and take on a world full of giants. You have shown me what uncompromising honesty and openness looks like. For me, our friendship has been the epitome of "iron sharpens iron."

Cornel – Charismaministries.org was the first new covenant based website I stumbled on. I got stuck on there for hours. The first article I read was *More Boldness? Do You Know What You Are Saying?* I was blown away. Boldness was one of the things I had been pursuing the hardest since I became a Christian, and in a few short paragraphs, you convinced me that I already had it. My life hasn't been the same ever since.

Paul – I haven't met you in person yet, but every time I've had a conversation with you or read something you've written, I can *feel* the grace of God overflowing from your heart into mine. You really know Him!

My Facebook Page – To those of you who have dared to ask questions and voice disagreements with me on a public forum, and those of you who have engaged in civil conversations with me—thank you for the mercy and grace you have shown me as I continue to grow and learn how to do life. I know my approach can sometimes be unconventional, and my ideas oftentimes unorthodox, but the very few of you who have stayed next to me regardless of disagreements, you have no idea how much that means to me.

Thank you for your endless support.

A special thanks to **Oliver-Kriel** for allowing me to use his picture on the cover of this book.

Table of Contents

Foreword

There's a story in this book about a pantry. I mention this because I love pantries. On a value-for-size basis, pantries must be the best room in any house. They are little treasure rooms full of secrets and goodies. In our house, the pantry is not just a storeroom for food. It's the place we keep our picnic gear, party supplies, unwrapped gifts, the first aid kit, and spare shoelaces. Our pantry is the answer to the question, "Where do we keep the good stuff?"

Jesus once said a teacher who knows something about the kingdom of heaven is like a householder who brings treasures out of his storeroom. Daniel Silva is that wise householder and his book, *It's All About Jesus*, is full of treasures from heaven's pantry.

Actually this book is more than that. It's an invitation for you to raid the pantry for yourself. It's the audacious boast that the pantry is unlocked so come, and take what you need. God's grace is for everyone.

When buying a book, many will turn to the back cover to read the author bio. They want to know, "Who wrote this and why should I listen to him?" Here's what you need to know about Daniel Silva: He likes to ask questions. Like a modern Søren Kierkegaard, Daniel looks at the religion many of us grew up with and asks, "Why?"

Questions are good. When we stop asking, we stop growing. Manmade religion would have you sit up and shut up and ask nothing, but the gospel Jesus revealed prompted questions. Jesus didn't mind questions; he welcomed them. In fact, he often asked questions of his own: "Who do you say I am?" "What is written and how do you read it?" Jesus asked questions to make people think because those who don't think don't change.

I love Daniel's questions. (I like his answers too.) I wish more people would ask the sorts of questions Daniel raises in this book for they are questions that open doors and demolish strongholds. They are questions that illuminate and liberate. And they are questions that will lead you to a deeper revelation of the greatest Answer of all.

Paul Ellis

Author of the forthcoming book, *The Gospel in Twenty Questions*

Preface

It's no secret by now that the American Church often finds itself bogged down by religious jargon, spiritual buzzwords, and a variety of rituals that completely miss the point of Christianity, which is, as Paul mentioned, Christ and what He did.

Much of what is presented as Christianity in America today actually has little, if anything to do with Christ; and that's often confusing for a lot of people.

For much of my Christian life I would go to church and all I would hear about was myself and my failures: how filthy I am, how much I sin, how much my sin separates me from God, how much I (present-tense) need His forgiveness, how much harder I need to try and get sin out of my life so God can be pleased with me, how much more I need to read my Bible, fast and pray, ask God to pour out His blessings on my life, etc.

All of those things have the appearance of spirituality, but much of it nullifies the work of The Spirit and ties burdens to our back that He's already carried. In other words, it's bondage in an appealing spiritual package, and as a result many people see the pretty bow and unwrap it without question.

What I wanted to emphasize the most when writing this book is how complete you already are in Christ. There's no more to get from God; there's only more to discover about what He's already given—then only more to enjoy.

When I finally learned that I didn't have to stress and strive for His approval, I was able to relax from the strenuous work of trying to become a good Christian, and I was able to just enjoy being.

For those who receive that rest which God promised will rest from their own work, just as God rested from his. (Heb. 4:10, NIV)

One of the major goals of my writing is to get people to ask questions. It's not merely to feed people a different type of food then they are getting from their pastors or drag them out of one belief system into another. It's to teach them how to feed themselves so they won't always need me or anyone else when they find themselves in a troublesome situation.

As the old saying goes, "give a man a fish and you feed him for a day. Teach a man to fish and you feed him for a lifetime."

I'm not here to merely give you the answers you're looking for; I'm here to teach you how to find those answers for yourself. That's what will benefit your life long after I'm gone.

I grew up in church, reliant upon pastors and friends to give me answers to all of my spiritual needs. Although it's not bad to have people who can help you with problems, it becomes an issue when you are completely helpless without them around.

I want to teach people how to stay fed and healthy even if their pastors and friends aren't around—even if they make that all important decision to stop attending church on Sunday. (gasp!)

Who This Book is For

Although I think anyone can get a lot of life-changing things out of this book, I mainly wrote it with the following people in mind:

- Those who feel like they've hit the dead-end of Christianity and don't know where to go next.

- Those who are tired of being hopelessly trapped in sin while being given no real answers on how to get out, besides "It's just your nature, there's no way to stop sinning until you die!"

- Those who are tired of struggling to obey the strenuous, man-made rules of modern Christianity.

- Those who are tired of constantly walking on eggshells around God, terrified of making a wrong move and disappointing Him (and thinking He abandons you in that disappointment).

- Those who have lost, or are losing all hope, and need relief from their wounds that they aren't finding anywhere else.

- Those who are willing to be honest with themselves about their frustrations, questions and doubts, and have not been able to do so without fear of being judged by their leaders and peers, being made to feel faithless and doubtful, or being given stock Christian answers that merely sweep the problems under the carpet.

- Those who can smile great in public, but in private they feel miserable, exhausted, and ready to give up.

I wrote this book for you because that was much of my Christian life as well. I didn't know what to do when I realized that a religion that promised me heaven only seemed to bring me a perpetual hell. I was made to believe that was the normal Christian life; then I heard the gospel.

The overall goal of this book is to restore your hope and help you enjoy the life you already have in Jesus, instead of being caught up in distraction after distraction, constantly running in circles trying to buy things through your own effort that you've already received through His.

Before you continue (and if you're willing to do so), I'd like you to place your hands over your heart and pray, "Eyes to see, ears to hear, and a heart to receive all of the good things Christ has already provided for me."

Amen.

I hope you find hope and encouragement in these pages.

When I first came to tell you about what God has achieved, I didn't try to win your applause with polished speeches and the latest impressive philosophy. I intentionally kept it simple: who Jesus is; what Jesus did—nothing more than Christ crucified! (1 Corinthians. 2:1-2, Personal Paraphrase)

An Expert's Guide to Burn-Out

"I love You, God!" I said, with desperation in my voice, "I know that will never change. But if this is the normal Christian life, then I don't want to be a Christian anymore!"

There it was, I was finally at the end of myself. Angry, depressed and quickly losing my will to live, I had stumbled upon one too many contradictions and hypocrisies in the faith I had devoted my life to.

One week I would hear people say, "Christ has set us free from sin," in the next I would hear, "We will always sin as long as we are in these bodies. Heaven is where we'll be set free from sin!" And in another, "Your sin separates you from God!"

The equation had come together and the sum of it was clear: Christ had set me free from sin, but I would continue to be controlled by it. Even though it was my nature to break the rules, I was still required to try my hardest to keep them. Even though God knew I couldn't keep them, He still expected me to try my hardest to, and was disappointed with me whenever I couldn't.

What was the "good news" part of the gospel again? Why did Jesus even bother coming in the first place? Was it merely to make the announcement that *someday* He would return to *really* help us?

The Gospel of Limitations

Is the message of the gospel really only limited to forgiveness of sins and heaven when you die?

God sent Jesus to die so I could be forgiven for my sins (on the condition that I ask for forgiveness for each individual sin I commit), and I can go to heaven when I die (on the condition that I've repeated that very specific rehearsed prayer at an altar call); however, I will never experience heaven while I'm alive because it will still be my nature to sin as long as I'm in this body that houses a wicked heart that constantly fails God. And because sin not only disappoints God but also separates me from God, I'm destined to be distant from a disappointed God every day of my life, either until I die or until Jesus returns and decides to zap me up to heaven.

What a cruel tease, don't you think?

Imagine I come upon a burning building with a ladder in my arms. I notice a panicked woman dangling helplessly over the fire-escape on the top floor and I'm the only one around who can help.

She's terrified and screaming, and her white dress is blowing so violently in the wind that the daffodils patterned across it appear to be floating away. Her sweaty fingers are slowly losing their grip as the fire spreads throughout her apartment and the pitch black smoke pours from her window straight into her lungs.

I yell up to her, "Don't worry, Mrs.! I heard your frantic cries for help and I've come here with my ladder to help you!"

"Oh, thank God!" she says, exhaling deeply as a small amount of anxiety and smoke leaves her chest, "I'm saved!"

"Thank God, indeed!" I reply, "You wouldn't have lasted much longer had I not come along! Just hang in there and try your hardest not to fall. Everything will be okay! I'll be back for you soon; I'm not sure of the day or the hour I'll return, but stay hopeful and remember: it's entirely up to you to hang on until I return!"

Ouch! And here she was thinking *today* was the day of her salvation.

For God only knows how many years, we've believed the lie that the sum of the gospel is that Jesus came to put a Band-Aid on an ancient problem while leaving the source of the problem completely untouched and intact, and the solution to the problem purposely withheld until an unknown day in the future (not even Jesus knows when that day is).

Yes, if you ask you can be forgiven for your sins. Yes, if you said the prayer you can go to heaven when you die. But as long as you're alive you're still a wretched sinner with a wicked heart who is prone to fail and disappoint God every day of your pitiful little life, and there's nothing you can do about it.

How in the world have we let that come across as the gospel for so long?

Do we even know that the word gospel means *glad-message*? Do we not realize that there is nothing *glad* about the message that has been presented as Christianity for so many years?

Yet, because we've invested so much of our lives into it it's like we have to deny all of the horrible implications of this message.

To admit that we've missed it means to admit that we've wasted our lives up until this point. And that is quite understandably a terrifying thought.

The Christian Product

Have you ever bought something expensive from the store, and when you got it home you realized that it's not anything like you expected? It's cheap, it doesn't do anything you thought it was going to do, and it looks nothing like it did on TV—it sucks, plain and simple. But because you paid so much money for it and you believed all the hype, you force yourself to enjoy it and make the best of it. You call your friends and tell them that it's the best thing you've ever owned in an attempt to convince yourself that you're getting what you paid for.

I've had a few friends do that when they've purchased video games. It's more than obvious that they hate every second they're playing that game, but they talk it up like it's the most entertaining and revolutionary game they've ever played. Why? Because they've hyped it up and hoped for so long that it would deliver on its promises, and they've invested so much of their time and money into it. If they don't comfort themselves with the continuous hype of how good it is, they will be forced to acknowledge the disappointing fact that they've been ripped off and lied to.

We do the same thing with the gospel.

It's more than obvious that people feel disappointed, ripped off and cheated because the *glad-message of the happy*

God (1 Tim. 1:11) has turned out to be nothing more than a mad-message of an angry God.

Yet because we've invested so much of our time and money into this thing, and we've hoped so much for it to deliver on its promises, we go on pretending that it's the best thing in the world. We tell friends and strangers how great it is and how much it has changed our lives.

Most of the time, we're not telling them what it actually is, we're telling them what we thought it would be when we signed up—the same thing people told us it would be when they got us to.

An honest Christian sales pitch would sound like this, "I used to be a worm, nothing but a rotten sinner, then I met Jesus and He completely changed my life! Now I'm a forgiven worm, a rotten, but forgiven, sinner!"

That product sounds great, right? You were once a certain type of person in need of help, but after receiving this revolutionary, life-changing product, you are now... the same type of person, in need of the same type of help.

You were a sinner prone to sin before Jesus, but after Jesus you became a forgiven sinner, *still* prone to sin. That is... revolutionary indeed.

Were we really waiting thousands of years for a Messiah just for the forgiveness of sins? Didn't people already have forgiveness through the sacrifice of bulls and goats? They did.

While I appreciate the fact that I don't have to sacrifice my pets to God every year, and I get to go to heaven when I die, the main issue was not that we were lacking forgiveness, but that we were lacking power against that slave-driving tyrant named Sin. We had no choice; we were destined to obey the commands of sin, no matter what we did.

Even though much of the Christian population proclaims their freedom from sin (according to Romans 6), they simultaneously declare that they are still sinners who can't escape sin's control (according to Romans 7).

Now be honest, does that really sound like freedom?

Forgiveness of sins is great, but I'd rather have the ability to quit doing the things I keep needing forgiveness for.

Subconscious Hypocrisy

Like countless others, I grew up in church quoting all of the famous Bible verses like, *We are no longer slaves to sin* (Rom. 6), and *Christ lives in me* (Gal. 2:20), but there was blatant hypocrisy involved in doing this since I spent every day expecting to sin by nature, striving to avoid sin, always pleading with Christ to come be with me, and thinking He separates Himself from me if I sinned.

In one breath I would say, "Jesus lives in me, I'm the temple of the Holy Spirit!" and in the next, "Come, Holy Spirit! We invite you into this place tonight!"

Never will I leave you nor forsake you looks great in a picture frame on the wall next to your front door, or on a magnet on your refrigerator, but a lot of people don't really believe it beyond a nice philosophy—not even the ones who quote it with tear-soaked passion and conviction.

I grew up hearing, believing and repeating things like "God cannot look upon sin, so when we sin we must repent and come back to God," because I was taught to believe that God comes and goes depending on how I behave. But how can that be? How can I return to someone I never left? *Never will I leave you nor forsake you,* remember? There was no asterisk or fine print under that promise.

I believe the main reason so many people speak and act as I did (in such a contradicting way) is because their foundation isn't built on Christ. While your foundation can still be perfectly built on verses and stories in scripture, if it's not built on the person of Christ, your foundation is no good, and will eventually fail you.

DIY (Do It Yourself) Theology

So many people build their foundation on their favorite scriptures and the lives of their favorite Bible heroes like Elijah, Elisha, David, Abraham, and others. We are taught to think that we are hearing "The Word of God" just because we hear a few references to people and events in the Bible, but we never realize that the book and the Person are not the same (*The Word became flesh* [John 1], not paper).

It's that kind of thinking that leads people to become confused, as they make one double-minded decision after the other getting tossed back and forth by the wind and waves, mindlessly accepting every new doctrine and jumping into every new movement that holds appeal.

For example, in much of the prayer movement we hear so much about Elijah, John the Baptist, Esther, the Nazarites, and how much we need to strive to resemble them and act as they did, but we don't hear very much about Christ and what He accomplished on the cross.

We don't hear about how we already resemble Jesus, and thus we will naturally act as He did if we believe (1 John 4:17, John 14:21).

We aren't told about how we were predestined to be conformed to the image of the Son (Romans 8:29), instead we are told to try and conform to the image of Old Testament prophets.

Week after week we hear the same depressing story of how Jesus died on the cross because we were naughty boys and girls who deserved (and according to many, still do deserve) to go to hell.

We hear descriptive details of the brutality of that day, and the imagery becomes so vivid in our heads and plays on our emotions to such an extent that by the time the altar call invitation in dropped on us, we would think ourselves to be heartless human beings if we didn't re/commit our lives to Him.

We are told of how the Father's patience had finally run out and how justice had to be served—which meant He had to pour out His entire cup of wrath on His creation. But, lo' behold! Jesus stepped in front of the bullet and took the entirety of God's wrath in our place. Now we're responsible to respect that display of love by trying harder than ever to keep God's commands (emphasis on The Ten).

We are taught to live in a way that says Jesus didn't come to take away the Law, He came to give us the power to obey it! But look at the following verse.

When you were dead in your sins and your sinful nature had not yet been removed, God made you alive with Christ. He forgave all our sins, and canceled the written law, with the regulations that stood against us; he took it away, and nailed it to the cross. (Col. 2:13-14, Personal Paraphrase)

Why did He take it away? Because it stood against the people.

Verse after verse in scripture speaks of how the Law brought judgment and death, increased sin, kept people in bondage, etc.

Jesus didn't come to empower people to obey the Law, He came to empower them to live free from it—outside of its restrictive walls that were closing in on us.

Beneath the super-spiritual guise of our prayers, our perspectives of God often sound like this: "Thank You Father for pulling the trigger, and thank You Jesus for taking the bullet from Father's gun. We owe You big time! We will try extra hard to keep your commandments from now on!"

Although Jesus and the cross get a shout-out every week, the overall emphasis in many sermons today is not on what He did for us, but on what we need to do for Him. "He died for me! The least I could do is sin less and read my Bible more. Gee whiz! I couldn't even take ten minutes of my day to pray? After what He did for me? I'm so unworthy!"

We've created programs and formulas for doing Christian chores, getting rid of our sin, appeasing God's wrath (which somehow returned after the cross), and drawing closer to Him, and yet how much of that actually changes our behavior long-term? Be honest, how has all of that been working out for you? (Albert Einstein has been quoted as saying insanity is doing the same thing over and over again and expecting different results. So how many times have you jumped through those same hoops expecting a different outcome? Are you exhausted enough to try something different?)

In one sense we have focused on everything we need to do, in another sense we have focused on everything He will eventually do when He returns, yet, in both senses we've completely ignored what He has already done. And because we are taught to stress and strive to accomplish what He already has, Christians are becoming increasingly more frustrated with their faith and burning out.

Make no mistake, sin has been dealt with once for all, and we are as close to Him as we will ever be.

It wasn't through our tedious efforts of prayer, fasting and intercession; it was through His sacrifice on the cross (1 John 2:2, 2 Cor. 6:17, Hebrews 10:12, 1 Peter 3:18). The question is not what will we do in order to attain holiness and closeness with God, but rather, what self-righteous attempts at holiness are we willing to give up in order to accept that we have already received holiness and closeness through *His* efforts?

Don't misunderstand me. People could be saying things that are one-hundred percent true about Elijah, John the Baptist, David, and the Nazarites. But if those stories and sermons don't find their eventual conclusion at the cross and the already finished work of Christ (bringing people into the knowledge of the fullness of Christ in them), those stories and sermons will always lead to a dead-end road of confusion and destruction. Those stories and sermons will never be the gospel—no matter how many superficial smiles you lay on top of it.

Everything Points to Jesus

When Christ said to build your house on the rock, He wasn't referring to Old Testament prophets, the Law, or even your favorite Bible verses. To build your house on those things is like building your house on shadows — they have no substance. When He said to build your house on the rock, He was referring to Himself.

Everything in scripture is meant to point us to Christ, nobody else.

You have your heads in your Bibles constantly because you think you'll find eternal life there. But you miss the forest for the trees. These Scriptures are all about me! And here I am, standing right before you, and you aren't willing to receive from me the life you say you want. (John 5:39, THE MESSAGE)

One of the major issues with the Pharisees was that they were so focused on a Christ-to-come that they completely missed the Christ-who-came, even though He was standing right in front of them. That's not to imply that anyone is a Pharisee, it's only to point out the similarity, in this regard, to much of the church today.

All of our talk is about what He will do when He gets here, how He will rescue us from sin and sickness when He returns, while completely ignoring what He has already done.

What says Christ doesn't return today and His most faithful followers don't turn around and have Him crucified again (if that were possible)? That's what happened the first time, after all.

The Pharisees knew everything there was to know about the Messiah. They had studied up on him for years (generations, in fact), and yet, it wasn't atheists, homosexuals, drunks, drug addicts or abortionists who put the Son of God on a cross, it was the self-proclaimed "followers of God" (the "Christians" of the day) who had been preparing for His arrival for a few millenniums.

Nothing New Under the Sun

They expected their Messiah to come and force their governmental enemies and oppressors to bow down to their religious laws and traditions. Instead He came and disrupted their religious laws and traditions and told them that they had missed the entire point of being God's people.

Sound familiar?

How often do we hear leaders trying to convince us that God needs to set the President straight? And that He will return and bring justice and punishment on all of our enemies and oppressors for the mistreatment we've received from modern day Gentiles for trying to force them to live by ancient Jewish laws?

The position the church is in is very similar to the position the religious leaders were in when Jesus first showed up.

There's a high chance that if Jesus returned today, many of His own followers wouldn't recognize Him; they wouldn't believe it was really Him.

They would label Him a heretic and a blasphemer. They would kick Him out of their churches, and slander him in books, blogs, and magazines. They would preach sermons about how He is bringing the end-times deception. They might even start telling their congregations that He is the Anti-Christ.

Just like Jesus told the religious leaders of His day, so many people in our day have their heads shoved so deep into the *words* of scripture, that they can't recognize the *person* those scriptures are all about.

It's Not About You

And while Paul did mention Christ's return, the overall emphasis of His letters wasn't on that. It was to bring the focus back to what Christ had already accomplished for us on the cross, and who we already are in Him. One of his most famous examples,

> ... *so that it is no longer I who live, but it is Christ who lives in me. This life that I live now, I live by faith in the Son of God, who loved me and gave his life for me. I refuse to reject the grace of God. But if a person is put right with God through the Law, it means that Christ died for nothing!* (Galatians 2:20-21)

Here's a personal paraphrase of that verse: *It's not about me and what I do or don't do! I'm the equivalent of dead! Now it's all about Christ alive in me, faith in what He did! If I could have become righteous through what I did (all of that rule-keeping nonsense) then there was no point in Christ doing what He did!*

See, we quote that verse in a celebratory tone all the time. I did for years, but I had no idea what it really meant. Outside of that text life was still all about me and what I did: how long I read the Bible, how many verses I memorized, how many consecutive minutes I prayed, what sins I did and didn't commit, etc. I was self-focused, and consequently self-condemned.

Verses like that one in Galatians are exciting to us because we were created to live a life completely caught up in that truth. But we simultaneously nullify the power that

Truth has to set us free by countering and contradicting it with our own man-made traditions (Mark 7:13).

If what we are feeding others or being fed ourselves is not pointing to Christ and His work, and is instead pointing to us and ours, then we have missed the entire point of the gospel.

The result is that we have people constantly church-hopping, going from conference to conference, always 'seeking' the presence of God but only being able to find Him at special Christian events.

They live from spiritual high to spiritual high, for those temporary feelings that only last as long as the hype, and then they have to go through it all over again.

By Feeling, Not By Faith

For the most part, people aren't actually seeking the presence of God, they are seeking that nice feeling—the spiritual and emotional high they get and have been taught to perceive as His presence.

Right now as I'm writing this, I don't feel anything! I have no tingles in my fingertips, no chills going down my back, and no swirling blizzard of heavenly gold dust is blowing through my apartment. Still, I know I'm in God's presence and I know He is here. I don't need a stadium-sized meeting, or guitar strings to be plucked beautifully alongside a hyped up call to arms in order to stir up my emotions so I can then be sure God is with me... or at least He is on His way.

Knowing Him is more reliable than feeling Him.

Think about it, does a husband need a dramatic build up from an orchestra to stir up feelings of love and desire for his wife? How about feelings of assurance that she loves him and is close to him? Will she only show him love if he sings her songs?

She said, "For better or worse, till death do us part." That was the promise that she's not going anywhere; I either believe her or I don't.

If my wife would only agree to come close to me on the condition that I create a special atmosphere every time I want to see her, then I think things would go downhill for us very quickly.

If God is Love, then He is the very definition of real love. Is love defined by what you do for me or what I do for you? If *love is not self-seeking*, then by default it is *others*-seeking, right?

Either you love me, or you don't. Either you want to be a benefit to me (and I to you), or you are only in it for what I can do for you and what kind of special atmospheres I can create to make you feel good about yourself—which is not true love, and certainly isn't God. Either it's unconditional like you tell me, or you're lying.

When He said He would never leave me, and that He would always be with me (Matt. 28:20), I believe Him, because He said it—that was His "till death do us part." And since we are alive for eternity, there will never be death, so there will never be a "do us part."

We pray things like, "God send Your presence! Rend the heavens and come down!" but His presence doesn't come and go, it's always here, wherever "here" may be. Do you remember what David said in Psalm 139:7?

I can never escape from your Spirit!

I can never get away from your presence!

If I go up to heaven, you are there;

if I go down to the grave, you are there.

If I ride the wings of the morning,

if I dwell by the farthest oceans,

even there your hand will guide me,

and your strength will support me. (NLT)

It's only our awareness of His presence that changes, not His actual location. Make yourself aware of Him right now, turn your affections towards Him and you'll feel His presence. That doesn't mean He suddenly jumps into the room (*"Surprise!"*), it's merely you realizing that He's already there.

He lives in you; His presence can never be very far from you.

His presence isn't released from the outside in; it's released from the inside out. We carry and release His presence and His Kingdom because both are contained inside of us (Luke 17:21). It isn't our job to call God's presence down, but to simply let it out for the world to experience.

But the person who is joined to the Lord is one spirit with him. (1 Cor. 6:17)

We are quite literally inseparable.

Now, don't get me wrong. I'm not against having good feelings. I do get them, and I do like them. I also know that husbands and wives do romantic things for each other all the time (we are made of pleasure sensors for a reason). However, the difference is in the idea of *requirement*.

Many believe that God *requires* a special atmosphere to be created before He can arrive. As if He's a prima donna who stubbornly refuses to step out of His white limo and walk into church unless somebody first rolls out the red carpet.

It's like the wife who refuses to acknowledge the husband unless he dims the lights, lights the candles, plays a few classic love songs and gets the "mood" right. It doesn't make for a healthy relationship.

Are there intimate times when the "mood" and the feelings are more intense? Absolutely! But those are not the only moments He is with you.

See, one of the key problems is that we don't always feel Him, and we've been taught to value feelings over faith (in my opinion, the word faith simply means confidence). If we don't feel something in a given moment we automatically conclude that it must not be a reality. On the contrary, if we do feel something, it *must* be a reality. If we feel distant, we *must be* distant; if we feel sinful, we *must be* sinful.

If we sin, we call that feeling of guilt the conviction of the Holy Spirit, thereby associating Him with wanting to make us feel bad if we break the rules. Yet, moments later we are quoting Romans 8:1, proudly declaring that *there is now no condemnation for those in Christ!*

We become confused because on one hand, there is no condemnation, and on the other we can't deny that we do get a feeling of condemnation if we sin. But rather than question whether we may be wrong about what we've been taught, we repackage condemnation, call it "conviction" (even though they're both synonyms of one another) and sell it in bulk to millions of believers.

The overall problems occur because our faith has become dependent on our feelings when it's meant to be dependent on His promises. That means that even if I'm not feeling close to Him, I stand my ground on the promise He made to never leave me or forsake me. If I start feeling condemned and guilty over sin, I stand my ground on His promise that there's no condemnation in Christ, and yes, as offended as some of you are about to get, there's no more guilt over sin either (Heb. 10:2).

Downward Spiral

Living by feelings is the quickest way to burn out. Feelings come and go, they waver and change. If you base your beliefs on experiential feelings, your beliefs will waver and change with your feelings, and neither your feelings nor your beliefs will ever be stable because of it.

One moment you will feel happy and complete because you feel Him there with you; but the very moment you cease to feel Him there, you start feeling empty—*maybe you did something to push Him away*—and you begin desperately begging for more of Him (even though you still have all of Him).

Nothing has changed between those two moments except for what you feel.

Living by feelings leaves you vulnerable as well. What if you start to believe what I believed for so many years: "God leaves me when I sin because He cannot look upon sin." As a result of believing it your feelings begin to line up with it. From then on if you sin, all of the sudden you feel empty and alone like God has lifted His hand from you. And now since you've felt it, you believe it to be true even more; you now have an experience that proves your new belief to be right. So then you fall even deeper into that belief, causing you to experience the feeling of it even more.

That goes on and on, over and over until you are spiritually, emotionally and mentally distressed and drained (perhaps even dead); all because you believed one little lie that said God leaves you when you sin.

Now combine that with another popular one that tells you that you can never stop sinning, and what do you get? A lethal mixture that says, "for as long as I live, God will always come and go, because I can never stop sinning and God cannot be around sin!"

Eventually you become convinced that you will only have those brief moments with God when you cry your eyes out at a repentance altar every few weeks, perhaps an extra pity-dose of God at the "cry out for the sins of the nation" conference once or twice every year.

You now know He can only come back to you and let you back to Him if you repent, confess each one of your sins, and make a heartfelt vow to quit being *so damn disappointing*! You may even have to take out your wallet every week and fork over the cash so He can continue blessing you.

Living that way quickly becomes a normal routine; over and over, day after day, week after week, month after month, and year after year. Nothing ever changes for more than a few days (a few weeks if you're lucky), but you have no other solutions so you have to keep coming back again.

It's an infallible money making machine when you have millions of people hooked on the "God feeling." Like the smoker who smokes to relieve stress, or the alcoholic who drinks to forget about his problems, people get addicted to the feeling they get from the product, and the industries get rich from convincing those people that they're the only ones who can supply the relief those people so desperately need.

A lot of people don't hesitate to pay for expensive stadium meetings or plane tickets to fly across the world, rushing to the latest self-proclaimed revival because they believe it's the only place to get their dose of God. We believe it isn't available anywhere else (at least not as potent).

But just like the alcoholic and the smoker, you're not actually fixing your problems by getting your dose; you're merely finding temporary relief from the problem in a temporary change of feeling. But the old feeling inevitably returns because the old problem still exists.

We feel so renewed after a good church service; super-renewed after a church getaway. But within a few days to a week we're right back in the rut we were in before: feeling empty and struggling to keep all those vows we made to God at the altar out of compulsion.

The issue isn't that God got bored with us and decided to leave, or that we're just incapable of doing anything right, it's that our faith is in the idea that He stayed in that stadium, or remained in that cabin we were in on the retreat. It's the idea that buildings are God's house when scripture says bodies are—namely, *yours*.

Why do you think we spend so much time looking forward to the next time we can go back to all of those places (church buildings, conferences, camps, etc.)? "The worship tonight was so good! I can't wait for next week!" We don't get to enjoy the moment because all of our time and focus is spent on searching for and anticipating getting more of the thing we've had all along.

Who Do You Think You Are?

Your broken promises and shortcomings don't fail or displease God. He isn't pleased with you based on what you do, He's pleased with you based on who you are. Your actions, good or bad, don't change who you are, they only reveal who you believe yourself to be. So the question is: who do you think you are?

If you think you're just a wretched sinner saved by grace, doomed and damned to sin every day, then you'll expect to fail God every day, every time you sin.

Since you were also taught you will sin for your entire life you already expect to fail God every day until you die. Hell, today isn't even over yet and you're already getting prepared to apologize for all of the failing you'll be doing tomorrow, probably all the way up into next week, too. You may have even already reserved a spot at the church altar next Sunday. Knock it off. Those things get passed off as the gospel, but they are far from *good* news, are they not?

If these things aren't dealt with, you eventually stop trying to find solutions to problems and just learn to accept that all of the junk is the "normal Christian life". When you tell the rest of your church group that your Christian life has been like an up and down roller-coaster, you immediately see the empathy on their faces, relieved to know that they aren't the only ones who go through it. Once again, they are reassured as well as you are that all of this is just the "normal" routine for a Christian—it will be until you die.

You've never met or heard of anyone who lives differently, probably not even your own pastor, so anyone who says they do is obviously lying.

I lived that way for years; no good ever came from it. It produces people who resemble starving orphans, going to "God's house" every week to beg for food, instead of people who reign in brilliance *as* God's house, enjoying the inheritance they have already received from their Father.

And that conveniently leads us to our next chapter. Have you been feeling hungry for God lately?

We Are Hungry, We Are Hungry

Jesus answered them and said, Most assuredly, I say to you, you seek Me, not because you saw the signs, but because you ate of the loaves and were filled. (John 6:26, NKJV)

Following the scene where Jesus feeds the thousands, we see some of those same people who were fed show up again, appearing anxious to see Him. However, Jesus calls them out and says they weren't seeking Him because of the signs (evidence of who He was), but because they got a nice feeling from Him the last time He was around—He filled them, and satisfied their hunger.

"I am hungry for more of His presence! I am thirsty to be filled! Only He can satisfy me!"

We've all said or sang something like that at one time or another. Most of us have probably been told of the importance of staying desperate, hungry, and thirsty for God. But let's think about that for a second.

Rich Dad or Poor Dad?

Assuming he is good, would a rich king ever leave his children desperate, hungry, and thirsty? Would he only feel motivated to feed them if they gathered together at his feet and begged for their daily bread (perhaps including statements of how 'unworthy' they are to be in his presence)? Or instead, since they are his children, and because he is rich and his resources cannot be exhausted, would his children not always be supplied with more than enough?

In a household that's on a tight budget, the refrigerator and pantry are usually off-limits to the children because parents don't want the children to eat everything in one day. If they wanted to open the fridge for a snack, the children must first check with mom and dad—sometimes even if it's just for a single package of string cheese.

However, in a household with a lot of income—the kind that always has a pantry stocked full of goodies—you will usually find that the children are more free to go in and eat at will, and they won't have to ask their parents each time they want to open the fridge, because there is plenty there to go around.

To the household on a tighter budget it may sound like the children in the wealthier household are brats and the parents irresponsible.

"They don't even ask their parents if they can eat the snacks? They are out of control!"

But there are fewer restrictions to snack-time in the latter household because snacks are not a luxury like they are in a household on a tight budget, so they don't have to be as heavily guarded. If the entire box of Twinkies (R.I.P.) disappears in one day, there are at least three more boxes backed up in the pantry.

When you come into your Father's kingdom, are you entering a household on a tight budget, or a household that has a pantry stocked full of goodies? Are His resources limited, or infinitely inexhaustible? So why do we act like beggarly children in a poor household who must beg Papa for a snack, instead of confidently opening the fridge and grabbing whatever we would like?

We think that's weird; rude even. "Grab whatever you like? Who do you think you are?" I'm His son, and because of that it's my house as much as it's His.

Now, it would be weird if we found the maidservant curled up in a corner of the pantry stuffing her face with Twinkies, or attempting to smuggle a box of Ho-Ho's out under her chocolate-covered apron. It's not her house, she doesn't even live there; she merely shows up once a week to serve, and then she leaves again to go about her life. She doesn't have the same rights to the fridge that a son has, and that is precisely the problem in much of the modern church.

People say they are sons, but believe they are servants, therefore they come before God like a timid servant asking for a raise instead of boldly approaching His throne like a son whose Father owns all things.

You are probably wondering how I can make such an absolute judgment like that, and it's simple: I'm looking at the fruit on the trees. People are proclaiming themselves to be sons but behaving as if they are servants. The fruit of what they believe about themselves speaks for itself. Your behavior will always reveal who you believe yourself to be in your heart.

As a man thinks in his heart, so is he. (Proverbs 23:7, NKJV)

Let's go back to John chapter 6 and we'll see that Jesus says something pretty amazing; something that would make a large portion of today's popular worship songs obsolete.

The people who were seeking Him said (referring to their physical hunger), "Give us more of this bread!" and Jesus replied in John 6:35 and addressed their spiritual hunger, saying, *I am the bread of life. Whoever comes to me will **never** go hungry, and whoever believes in me will **never** be thirsty.* (NIV)

Here's how Webster's dictionary defines the word *never*:

1. not ever : at no time

2. not in any degree : not under any condition

So let's try this again.

*I am the bread of life. Whoever comes to me will **not ever, at no time, in any degree, under any condition** go hungry, and whoever believes in me will **not ever, at no time, in any degree, under any condition** be thirsty.*

The Ancient Problem

I want to point out something ironic. In the Old Testament when the people were wandering in the desert, they were constantly praying, "More, God, more! We're hungry and thirsty, give us more!" In the book of Hebrews it says that those same people died there because of their disobedience—which in context refers to their refusal to acknowledge and rest in what God had already provided for them (the food, water, miracles, and freedom from slavery).

Fast-forward to today and you see people who write songs and preach sermons about being in the "desert place," comparing themselves and their situations to those people in the wilderness. Worship songs and prayers are constantly filled with desperate cries that say, "More, God, more! We're hungry and we're thirsty, give us more!"

Here's my question: if the result of behaving that way before was people perishing, what makes us think the result of behaving that way now will be people receiving life? It's the same exact disobedience that killed off the Israelites in the desert: the refusal to acknowledge and rest in what God has already provided (the fullness of Himself to His entire creation).

Hebrews 4 says to learn from their mistakes so we don't end up following them and making the same mistake they did, which led to death. Yet, when you look around at much of the church today, the majority of people are blatantly making that same exact mistake (in ignorance, of course), thinking it will bring them life.

What's essentially taking place is that millions of people are blindly walking through an imaginary desert that only exists in their mind, searching for life but heading for death.

The devil is not as creative or as smart as I've given him credit for in the past. He seems to have one trick that has been repeated in various ways since the beginning.

"I know God said He gave you all of this awesome stuff, but trust me, He's been holding out on you. There's still a lot more to get!"

It's a different variant of the lie Adam and Eve fell for in the Garden. We've been made to believe that God is keeping the goods from us when He has freely given us everything we need.

It's been seen throughout the entire history of the world—man is always exerting all of his own effort into getting more of something, when God, in His effort, has given man everything.

You say, "Why, that's preposterous! Why would the devil want us to ask God for more?" Well, if we spend our lives seeking more, we will spend our lives ignoring everything we have already been given. The moment we acknowledge what has been given, as many of our Christian heroes in the past have done, it's more than enough to destroy all of the devil's work. The question is not why would he? But rather, why wouldn't he? Why not keep us distracted and thinking we are seeking God, when in reality we're not? They called him crafty for a reason.

But I am afraid that just as Eve was deceived by the Serpent's cunning, your minds may somehow be led astray from your sincere and pure devotion to Christ. For if someone comes to you and preaches a Jesus other than the Jesus we preached, or if you receive a different spirit from the one you received, or a different gospel from the one you accepted, you put up with it easily enough. (2 Cor. 11:3-6, NIV)

So here is the question: if Christians have come to Him, and have believed in Him, how can they still hunger and thirst for Him if He said they never would again? Could it be that they don't know what they have, and nobody is telling them?

That's what I believe.

Multiple Fillings

"Well see, brother, there are multiple fillings! We leak! We need to be continuously filled!"

People say that, yes, but what did Jesus say? He is addressing that very idea in John 6. As the people said, "We ate, we were filled, we had a nice bathroom break, and now we're hungry again. So do that thing you did last time because we need a second filling!" Had Jesus done His "magic trick" for them again, what would have happened? They would have come back the very next day wanting to be filled again.

Jesus combats the idea of temporary satisfaction and tells them, Listen, I'm not here to temporarily fill you up over and over! Anyone who comes to me will never hunger or thirst again, because I will fill them once and for all.

If you are merely looking for a temporary filling, you are better off spending your Sunday mornings at Krispy Kreme. Jesus isn't in the business of temporary filling. He wants you to be full forever so you never have to hunger or thirst for His Spirit again, and He never has to hunger or thirst for yours again either. We are one.

Do you need more air? No, you already have it. You can only be desperate for something that you don't already have. If I say, "I really need milk for my cereal," the automatic implication is that I don't already have it, or at the very least, I haven't checked the fridge. When people say, "I need more of God in my life," the implication is that they don't have Him, or at least not all of Him.

Would you say you have Him? If so, how much of Him do you have? Let's look at what scripture says (pay attention the usage of past-tense).

For out of His fullness (abundance) we have all received [all had a share and we were all supplied with] one grace after another and spiritual blessing upon spiritual blessing and even favor upon favor and gift [heaped] upon gift. (John 1:16, AMP)

In Christ, God has given us every spiritual blessing in heaven. (Eph. 1:3, ERV)

His divine power has given us everything we need for a godly life through our knowledge of him who called us by his own glory and goodness. (2 Peter 1:3, NIV)

For in Him the whole fullness of Deity (the Godhead) continues to dwell in bodily form [giving complete expression of the divine nature]. And you are in Him, made full and having come to fullness of life [in Christ you too are filled with the Godhead--Father, Son and Holy Spirit--and reach full spiritual stature]. (Col. 2:9-10, AMP)

I don't need to hunger for more of Him because I know I have all of Him. The only "hunger" is for more knowledge of what I already have so I can be more and more empowered to help others. It's a hunger to discover and enjoy what I already have, not a hunger for what I still need.

Stay Hungry and Thirsty

Pastors who I love and respect have emphasized how important it is that we stay hungry and thirsty for God. Of course, I always just took their word for it because... well duh! They're pastors, I'm not. They have the degrees, I don't. They spent a few years in Bible school, I haven't. They obviously know better than I do (or so I believed). And because I listened to them, I would often strain and strive during worship, expressing my hunger to God.

I would sing loud and obnoxiously off-key, stretch my arms into the air as high as they could go, while standing on my tippy-toes to gain that extra inch towards heaven (like a self-operated spiritual torture rack). I would jump up and down which would inevitably turn into dancing like a madman, and I would loudly and desperately proclaim, "Jesus! I'm so hungry for you! I need more of you! More, Lord! More! Come be with me! You're all I want!"

I didn't care who watched, or who laughed. Nobody and their opinions would keep me from getting what I 'needed.' I was desperate, yet at the same time, I was oblivious to the fact that the very thing I was desperately reaching up to heaven for had already come down from heaven into my heart.

The fruit of a lot of our sermons, prayers, and efforts is oftentimes only hunger and striving to do more and get more, when there is no more to get no matter how much we do.

The "more" of Christianity is a myth; a deceitful illusion designed to keep you busy and running in circles, always seeking but never finding, always learning but never coming to the knowledge of the Truth—a carrot on a stick, if you will.

If we so believe that Christ lives in our hearts, why are we always crying up to heaven to get Him to come down? If we so believe that we no longer live, why are all of our prayers and sermons about how much we are alive (how much we sin, fail, and disappoint God every day)? That's not the fruit of belief in those verses, that's the fruit of unbelief. And that's nobody's fault, and to nobody's shame, that's just what we've been taught.

Nobody had told me that I already had all of Him, and that all of those spiritual stretches and exercises I was doing didn't do anything except wear me out. I was already filled with Him, He was always with me, and He already promised He would never leave. He wasn't on the outside waiting for me to invite Him in, but on the inside waiting for me to invite Him out.

What do you do after you eat a good meal and become full? Do you go back and stuff as much food in your mouth as you think will fit? Or do you sit down, sink into the couch and relax? You relax, right? Because even if there was more food, there's nowhere in your belly for it to fit—hence the term, "I'm full," or "I'm stuffed." Likewise, if we are filled (or stuffed) with God, how can we continue to seek more of God? The only way is if we don't really believe we are already filled with Him.

Let me put this another way. Do you remember pie-charts in school? They were used to help us learn fractions, and they basically work like this: let's say 25% (or one quarter) of the people in a room like pizza for lunch, another 25% like spaghetti, and the rest of the people in the room like macaroni. What percentage of the people in the room like macaroni? The answer is 50%, right? How do we figure that out? Because 25% of the people like pizza, and another 25% like spaghetti, that takes up 50% of the people in the room (or one side of the pie). So the only people left in the room who can like macaroni in this equation are the remaining 50% (the other side of the pie).

Now suppose we write an equation like this: "If Christians have received 100% of God, what percentage of God is left for Christians to get?"

If you said 0%, you are absolutely right—you little mathematician, you! There's nothing left. We have the whole pie, now all we can do is sit down, sink in, relax, and enjoy it.

Christ has filled our entire being—every corner, every crevice and every pore. There is nowhere in us that He is not, and consequently there is nowhere in us that darkness is. Since we are full of Him, there is no room for anyone else. All of my efforts to get more of Him in and more darkness out are all in vain, because if I'm full of light, I'm already vacant of darkness.

I didn't learn what it means to be filled with Him until 18 years after I had become a Christian. Some people don't learn it until 30 years after, maybe 50, maybe 70, maybe never. They live their entire lives trying to get more of God, and as a result they are never able to sit down, relax, and enjoy the all of Him they already have. They are constantly sweating and slaving away over a hot oven, trying to prepare something to eat that will never fit into their bellies because their bellies are already full, they just don't know it.

Would you agree with me that it's a blatant rip off to live that way? It was very damaging to my life and the lives of a lot of other people I've met when we lived our lives that way.

What if our favorite revivalists weren't the way they were because they cried out night and day for more of God and He finally gave in and quit withholding His Spirit from them? What if they were the way they were because they came to the realization that they already had all of Him? In realizing that they had all of Him, they realized that revival is not a once-in-a-generation event that comes from a specially anointed individual who climbed to the top of the pyramid, but rather, revival is meant to be an ongoing lifestyle lived throughout every generation, carried by every individual person—a level playing field.

What if no one is greater, more blessed, or more anointed than you are? What if Paul was right when he said we are all one (equal) in Christ? What if those heroes of the faith that we look up to didn't actually have more of God than we do, they just knew something we don't?

We are awakening to that marvelous truth, that Christ is not in the heavens only, nor the atmosphere only, but Christ is in you. – John G. Lake

The Purpose of Pastors

I believe one of the major causes of problems in the church today is that the pastors, prophets, apostles, evangelists, and teachers who were entrusted to build up the body, don't actually know what it means to build the body up.

Build up the body often comes off like another one of those meaningless phrases in the vast collection of Christian clichés that get carelessly tossed around.

And He Himself gave some to be apostles, some prophets, some evangelists, and some pastors and teachers... (Eph. 4:11)

Here we see Paul list what people call the five-fold ministry: apostles, prophets, evangelists, pastors, and teachers. He then he goes on to tell us what their function is; their job description, so to speak.

And He himself gave some... for the equipping of the saints for the work of ministry, for the edifying (building up) of the body of Christ, till we all come to the unity of the faith and of the knowledge of the Son of God, to a perfect man, to the measure of the stature of the fullness of Christ; that we should no longer be children, tossed to and fro and carried about with every wind of doctrine, by the trickery of men, in the cunning craftiness of deceitful plotting, but, speaking the truth in love, may grow up in all things into Him who is the head-Christ, from whom the whole body, joined and knit together by what every joint supplies, according to the effective working by which every part does its share, causes growth of the body for the edifying of itself in love. (Eph. 4:11-16)

So we can see there that the purpose of the five-fold ministry is to equip the saints for the work of ministry. In one sense, it has worked. As far as numbers are concerned, the church has been turning out countless pastors and street ministers for centuries; as far as seeing a massive movement of people living like Jesus? Not so much (so far).

... for the edifying (building up) of the body of Christ...

This is where people like to stop and focus. But because they stop at an out of context phrase, *build up the body*, they end up doing what that they think is building up the body, but is actually hindering the body from being built up at all.

When confronting a lot of the things we are talking about in this book, I've frequently been told things like, "Let's stop this confrontation stuff and just build-up the body." Meanwhile, I was actually in the middle of building up the body before I was interrupted by somebody who doesn't know what building up the body means.

In the context that a lot of people say "build up the body," it often gives the impression that building up the body means to only say the warm, fluffy things that make people feel good. Never correct hurtful ideas or imply that somebody's beliefs are hurting themselves and others, only focus on the positive things about people and tell them how great they are!

I'm not against giving people compliments and letting them know how great they are, but that's not actually what building up the body means. Thinking that's what it means actually hurts more people than it helps. But let's keep going further into these verses.

... until we all come to the unity of the faith and of the knowledge of the Son of God, to a perfect man, to the measure of the stature of the fullness of Christ...

There we see the purpose of building up the body—it's that job description: to bring us all to the unity of the faith, and of the knowledge of the Son of God. It doesn't mean we don't confront bad theology; it means that we do! We confront anything that hinders unity of the faith and the knowledge of the son of God (although, learn from my mistakes, that doesn't mean to be a trigger-happy theology cop).

We demolish arguments and every pretension that sets itself up against the knowledge of God, and we take captive every thought to make it obedient to Christ. (2 Cor. 10:5, NIV)

When I see something that is distorting somebody's knowledge of God, I want to help them. Not because I want them to know I'm right and they're wrong, but because I want to bring them into a greater knowledge of Christ, helping them to mature to that perfect man, and to the measure of the fullness of Christ.

Independence

I believe the job of a pastor is to show you how to have relationship with Christ on your own so you are no longer dependent on him (the pastor) to breastfeed you every week. It's to build you up in the knowledge of who you are in Christ and who Christ is in you, so that you can function on your own and carry out the work of ministry with great effect. Afterwards you will be well equipped to help build others up into that same knowledge that you received, and then they do the same for others, and so on.

That's how Jesus worked with the disciples, and it's how the disciples worked with the churches they planted. They were fruitful, and they multiplied.

Just as God told Adam and Eve in the Garden concerning the sons of men, Jesus told the disciples concerning the sons of God, "Make disciples of all nations." His disciples made more disciples and built them up in the knowledge of Truth and the fullness in Christ, and they left their new disciples when they were confident they could walk on their own.

Many of Paul's letters were written to churches he had established who had heard the true gospel from him, but "backslid" into other things after he left. His letters, though full of encouraging words, were not all icing and no cake. The main objective of most of his letters was to correct errors and to help them get back to where they were when he was with them.

Unfortunately today, many pastors never get past the basics of the gospel in their sermons, so the people in their pews never have a real opportunity to grow up and learn to function on their own, and are therefore ill-equipped to teach others and bring them into the knowledge of Christ.

That lack of knowledge leads to many people making God out to be a boogie man, and threatening everyone with hellfire for the slightest hint of unbelief or sin. When they do teach others it often spreads damaging lies that enslave, rather than Truth that sets free.

Like those many churches Paul wrote to, many Christians today have no idea how to function without their pastor telling them what to read, how to pray, what to pray for, what songs to sing, etc. Like infants, many are completely helpless on their own.

It's not a new problem, either.

By this time you ought to be teachers yourselves, yet here I find you need someone to sit down with you and go over the basics on God again, starting from square one-baby's milk, when you should have been on solid food long ago! (Heb. 5:12, The Message)

A lot of Christians today are preaching somebody else's relationship with Christ, not their own. Oftentimes only repeating other people's sermons word for word.

If everything you know about Christ is based on "My pastor said…" then it's time to change some things around (and the entire point of this book is to help you do that). However, if the above does apply to you, don't feel ashamed or stupid over it. The vast majority of us have been through it.

As a side note, I still find areas where I realize I never actually looked into a doctrine for myself. I just took someone's word for it that the soil was good and started planting on top of it.

That's okay. We're growing and learning how to do life. There's no shame or guilt in being wrong, or in realizing that you've naively believed everything you've been told. In fact, when you give yourself grace to learn (by understanding that you are still learning and it's okay to mess up), it becomes exciting to find out where you're wrong about something. You quit seeing it as a moment of humiliation (and therefore don't get easily offended by it) and instead start seeing it as another opportunity to grow and learn something new.

I used to not be able to have a conversation about Jesus without quoting Bill Johnson at least once in every paragraph. Every time somebody asked me what I thought of something, I would immediately start my reply by saying, "Well, I really like what Bill Johnson said about this..." and then I would go on to quote one of his many fantastic one-liners (sometimes a large portion of one of his sermons).

There's nothing wrong with having heroes or looking up to certain pastors and quoting them. But again, if everything you know about Christ is only based on "My pastor said..." then it's obvious that you have been missing out on your own personal relationship with Jesus. If I ask you what you think about something, I'm interested in what *you* think about it, not what your pastor thinks.

I see that same thing happen all the time. When I would discuss disagreements with Calvinists, most of the replies to my questions were, "Charles Spurgeon says..." or, "John Piper says..." and again, it's perfectly fine to quote those guys, but regardless of everything they say, we have to ask ourselves, *What did Jesus say?* and then, "Does what I'm quoting from this man or woman actually even agree with Him?"

As much as I could quote Bill Johnson, Charles Spurgeon, John Piper, and countless others, I follow Jesus, not them. I want to know Jesus more than I know them. In order to do that, I have to learn to feed myself instead of relying on them to feed me.

Feed Yourself

I haven't consistently been to a church service in almost three years. In those three years I've grown more than I ever did when I was consistently going. (I'm still amazed by how that works.)

The common response when you tell someone you don't go to church is, first they look a little taken back and disappointed, and then they ask with a concerned tone, "Well how are you getting fed?"

Okay. Here's my secret. It might be a bit strange, maybe a bit unorthodox, perhaps even a little controversial, but it's really easy, and anybody can do it. It's quite possibly a million dollar secret, but I'm going to give it you at a heavy discount. Are you ready? Here it is.

My secret to getting fed outside of church is the same as my secret to feeding myself breakfast in the morning: I lift the spoon up to my mouth and I take a bite.

"That's it?"

Yes. That is it.

I read the Bible for myself, I interpret for myself, I discuss my ideas, opinions, questions and perspectives with my friends, I talk to God about those things, and most importantly, I'm willing to be wrong if anybody can prove it. The reason I say that's most important is because if you're not willing to be wrong, it doesn't matter how much you talk to God, you'll inevitably end up arguing with Him (and a lot of other people) about how right you are.

Someone will gasp at that and say, "I would never do such a thing to God!"

Ah! But remember, that's exactly what Peter said; then he heard the rooster crow, followed by the voice of Jesus in the distance saying, "Told ya so, Pete!" (Okay, maybe not that last part).

Imagine if every morning I had to wait for somebody else to feed me. I probably wouldn't ever get fed. Or I would only get fed when another person was available to feed me, and that's no good.

It's better to be able to eat when we are hungry, not just when it fits into somebody else's job description or schedule, right?

Unfortunately, many of us have ended up just like the Israelites who chose only to relate to God through Moses. "You go talk to God for us and tell us what He says..." That's how many people anticipate their weekly church services.

During the week the Pastor goes up the mountain and spends solitary time with God, collecting knowledge for his sermon, and once a week he comes down to talk to the people and tell them what "God said."

Likewise, during that week, most people are just going about their lives (some even building beautiful golden calves), and once a week the people say, "It's that time again! Let's gather and listen to our pastor tell us the awesome things God has to say to us this week!"

That mindset defeats the whole purpose of the cross, which was to bring man back into direct relationship with the Father through faith in Christ. They would no longer have to put faith in prophets and pastors to deliver messages to them because now they could interact with Him themselves on a personal level.

Christ is the intermediary between man and God, not your pastor.

You can hear God talk to you as well as any pastor or prophet, no extra 'anointing' required. Many people wait for God to communicate with them through outside signs and voices when it's all about Christ in you (Col. 1:27).

In the past God spoke to our forefathers through the prophets *at many times and in various ways,* **but in these last days** he *has spoken to us by his Son.* (Heb. 1:1, NIV)

Where is His Son? In you. So where is His voice?

Fluff vs. Substance

See, building the body up and giving the body nice encouraging compliments isn't always the same thing. I can say as many nice things as I want about someone, but if those nice things are not bringing them into a happier life through a better knowledge of the fullness of Christ *in them*, then I'm still only speaking empty words that will never satisfy that "hunger" they always feel.

I can't tell you how many times I've confronted someone on something they were saying, and somebody else jumps in and says, "Y'know, I just don't sense a spirit of love in this." (As if their love detector is the only one that matters.) "We need to stop all of this bickering and just build people up!" What they are often implying is "You're not catering to their feelings enough, and by insinuating that they are wrong you are making them feel bad!"

The thing with that is He never said, *You shall know good feelings, and good feelings will set you free!* He said, *You shall know the Truth, and the Truth shall set you free.*

I'm by no means one of those people who thinks if you're not being rude and hurting people's feeling with your message, then you're only preaching a watered-down gospel, but I'd rather people know Him and be free, than to know a giddy feeling that only lasts as long as the compliments remain new and exciting. Because once the giddy feeling from nice compliments goes away, that person runs to the next conference to get another "encouraging word" from the celebrity prophet just to make themselves feel better and more secure, even though they've never even established themselves in the first encouraging word they received.

The dangerous part about that is you become an easy target for manipulative marketing. People can easily sell you on the next conference, book and DVD, even if it's no different than the last conference, book and DVD you spent your money on.

It goes back to being hooked on a feeling. When you are, you will pay top dollar over and over again in pursuit of a feeling that goes away soon after the conference ends, the book is finished, or the DVD is watched. And when the novelty from one wears off, they just rephrase a few of the same points they made before, retitle the book, change the name of the conference, get a new cover for their DVD, and put it all out in the market again. Like clockwork.

Don't trust any system that only gives you small tastes and teases of something, and promises you more if you keep coming back. That's how drug dealers work. They only give you enough to get you addicted, and then once you are they have you wrapped around their finger because they "hold the supply."

I've been watching churches operate like drug dealers for ten years. "Come out to our meeting and experience the presence of GOD." And yet, we're never taught how to experience God outside of the temple, so we have to keep going back and paying our tithes for that weekly dose.

It's manipulation—an easy way to build a ministry. It works out great for the guys at the top of the pyramid, but it's not how Jesus did it.

The lie is that if you quit going to those meetings you won't be able to get your fix anymore. But remember: God is *everywhere*, not just in church buildings. You can experience him on a bar stool just as much as you can in a pew.

Test Everything

If we were totally honest, we probably rarely, if ever, check to see if the last prophetic word we received was even accurate according to scripture. It just vaguely applied to our lives, resulting in a *oh my God!* moment, and therefore we bought it without question.

I'm not against prophetic words. I know they can be accurate, encouraging, and change a person's entire life, but we have to start testing everything we hear and tossing out everything that doesn't point to Christ, regardless of the many critics who will call it dishonoring because so much of it disagrees with the guys at the top.

The first prophetic word I ever received as a Christian was in 2003, it went something like this, "God wants to bring you overseas to do missions in Asia." (Oh that's already exciting, every Christian wants to do missions!) "He is preparing you for that right now... but if you go there before He is through preparing you, you will die!" (Strong emphasis on the die part.)

I didn't line that up with anything in scripture, I didn't even check with God to see if it was even Him. I just received it because it appealed to something I wanted to do (the missions, not the dying), and I said, "Wow! Thanks for the word, God!"

I bit, chewed, and swallowed, no questions asked. And for years afterwards, whenever I would so much as *think* of going overseas for anything (even non-Christian adventures), I would have that haunting voice pop up in my head and remind me, "What if you're not prepared yet and you get killed?"

That word, though sub-consciously traumatizing (causing me to be paralyzed by the thought of going overseas), made me feel good when I received it. It made me feel included. Wow! God really wants to talk to me! Which He does, but I never double-checked to see if it was actually His voice I was hearing through the words of that small woman with good intentions.

We are trained to live from good feeling to good feeling instead of from Truth. We aren't taught to "test everything and hold to what is good," we are taught to test some things, and only hold to what makes us feel good. That's a major source of dysfunction in churches and Christians throughout the world.

The whole problem begins in that we have goodhearted, well-intentioned pastors, prophets, evangelists, apostles, and teachers who don't know what their duty is, and who don't have the knowledge of the fullness of Christ in them.

While they can give people well-polished sermons, produce hyped-up emotions, nice compliments, and help people use their imaginations by sharing visions and prophecies, they still can't build people up into the knowledge of the fullness of Christ, because they don't have it themselves.

Moving Backwards

Out of the overflow of the heart, the mouth speaks. (Matthew 12:34)

Unfortunately, many people speak more about Joseph, Elijah, Elisha, and all of the Old Testament heroes than they do about Christ, who is the center of our faith and the promised land destination of the entire Old Testament.

Every single Old Testament prophet, preacher and story in the Bible is pointing to Christ, not itself. Jesus said, *These scriptures are all about me*, yet today we point everybody back to those prophets, preachers, and stories as if they are the substance, and then we get confused about why people are so confused.

An arrow is not the substance of a destination it merely shows you the way to get there; it points you in the right direction. Many have been taught to leave the destination, go all the way back to the arrow, and excitedly anticipate an eventual arrival at... the destination. How counter-productive is that?

Yet this future-tense preaching continues with no present-tense results, as people continue to file into buildings to cheer for it again and again. The entire time we are being given empty promise after empty promise, year after year.

"It's around the corner!"

"It's on the horizon!"

"I see it in the distance!"

No you don't, because it isn't around the corner, it isn't on the horizon, and it isn't in the distance. It's here; right now.

Do you not say, 'Four months more, and then the harvest'? I tell you, open your eyes and look at the fields! They are ripe for harvest! (John 4:35, NIV)

I tell you, now is the time of God's favor, now is the day of salvation. (2 Cor. 6:2, NIV)

However, if I can push people's expectations for results into the future, then I'm free from any responsibility to produce results in the present, and that's exactly what goes on.

We wash our hands of "sinners" and blame them for darkness, while neglecting our responsibility as the light. It's not the darkness's fault that it's dark, that's its nature, but if a light is placed into a dark place and that place remains dark, there's something wrong with the light for not doing what it was created to do (and I don't say that in a scolding or condemning way).

You Are Complete

New Christians are full of light and are consistently "on-fire" because they've arrived at their destination: relationship with Christ. It's all they know. Then what happens?

"Oh no, brother, there are still things you need to do, roads you have to travel, turns you have to take before you really arrive at your destination and become holy." (Gee, that voice sounds familiar, doesn't it?)

People say things like, "I used to be zealous like you, and then I grew up and calmed down!" So, not knowing any better (and being surrounded by so many people who took a bite of that same apple), newer Christians just buy into that stuff and expect to calm down the more they grow. And since they put faith in it, they inevitably experience it— it's not long until they fall in line with everybody else. Then they spend the rest of their life searching for that destination, striving and working to get there when they were already there to begin with, but got talked into leaving by good-intentions and carnal knowledge.

Do you see the point?

You can say nice things to other Christians as much as you want and still not be building them up in unity, faith, and the knowledge of Christ. In fact, you can say nice things and be teaching them *out* of unity, faith, and the knowledge of Christ. To build the body up means to bring the body into the knowledge of its fullness in Christ—nothing more, nothing less.

For in Christ all the fullness of the Deity lives in bodily form, and you have been given fullness in Christ. (Col. 2:9-10)

We will start manifesting that reality as we acknowledge all of the good things that are already within us in Christ (Philemon 1:6).

Proper Purpose

We have been so conditioned to think that "Church" is only a place where we go to sing a few songs and hear a guy make a few relevant spiritual points that fill our spiritual bellies once or twice a week. But it's amazing how rapidly I began to grow when I stopped relying on the pastor to fly the airplane into my mouth and instead picked up the spoon and started feeding myself.

However, let me be clear that I'm not against pastors or churches, or going to churches and learning from pastors. But it's vitally important to the Body that pastors serve their proper purpose.

I don't play baseball and try to swing a bat with my feet, or worse yet, try to hit the ball with my head. Neither my feet nor my head would serve the purpose of moving me forward in that game (at least not when trying to hit the ball). However, in a game of soccer my feet and my head would serve a greater purpose than my hands and arms would. Likewise it's important that pastors know what their purpose is for the role that they are in, and that they know how to properly serve that purpose so that the entire team can move forward.

I'm not at all implying that your pastor is useless and you should never listen to him. I'm saying that if your pastor decides to go out there and try to head-butt a baseball, you have to have learned enough about the sport on your own to not go out there and imitate him.

Some of your team will call you dishonoring, rebellious, or any number of things for not going along with your pastor and playing ball like he did, but that's okay, you're not in the wrong; you're sticking to what you know is right (and protecting yourself in the process).

In the next chapter I want to tackle one of the more popular ideas in Christianity. That is the idea of "mystery."

The Mystery of God Revealed

I grew up in a Christian environment, and for much of my life I've gotten the amazing opportunity to learn and experience how a large majority of Christians deal with tough situations; whether it be losing a loved one, a job, a house, a car, or any of the numerous, troublesome things that happen in life.

It isn't uncommon to see a devout Christian fall back on very popular quotes and catch phrases, often sounding like they were ripped straight from a bumper sticker. One of the most famous Christian catch-phrases we have is, "God works in mysterious ways!"

By the time I was in a situation of losing a closed loved one, I had different thoughts about that quote. But in the past I have used that one (albeit different versions of it) whenever somebody else lost a loved one or I ended up in a situation that didn't turn out as I expected.

While that quote did help me to feel secure about the problems I was facing, it eventually felt like a false sense of security that didn't really give me any kind of solution to my problem.

As long as we attribute tragedy and hardship to God's "mysterious work," we will never actually feel compelled to do anything about tragedies and hardships (not to mention how it makes us subconsciously feel towards God). We will never care to about learn how or why those things continue to happen in people's lives, instead we will settle down and accept that they are inevitable circumstances and there's not much we can do to prevent them.

It's the same common result that comes from another very famous one-liner, "God is in control!"

If I think that anything bad that happens is God being in control and working in a mysterious way that I can't understand, then all I can really do about my bad situation is accept it. I'm at the mercy of God, and whenever He finally decides to turn my situation around, He will. But until then (if then) I'll just have to put up with whatever He's given me, shouting my faithful amens and hallelujahs in the meantime.

Nowadays that's called having faith, yet the faith we see from Christ and the Apostles in scripture was active and aggressive towards the things that were hurting others; it wasn't apathetic and passive. It more often changed the bad situation than excused and tolerated it.

But of course, the key point there is that they viewed those things as the enemy, not as God. If they had viewed it as God, they might have just reacted like many of us do today, because nobody in their right mind would resist what they believe to be "God's will." If His will is for me to have cancer, I better just sit back and make the best of His gift.

God Allows Tragedy for a Reason

I've heard popular Church leaders teach their congregations that mystery is required for faith, and that we aren't supposed to understand every part of God, because if we could, we wouldn't need faith. It reminds me of what people have told me about why some get cancer.

"Clearly God allowed this because it drew people closer to God. Do you know how many people were touched by that person's story before he died? If he hadn't gotten cancer, that wouldn't have happened!"

While I understand this kind of reasoning (I used to reason that way myself), it implies that God isn't completely good, which is the main reason I resist those kinds of ideas. It implies that we are disposable to God and He is willing to kill any one of us (or allow us to be killed) if that means the rest of us who are still alive might give Him a little more attention.

After 9/11 happened, the churches were packed out the door for a week or two. The natural conclusion many of our famous church leaders came to at the time was that God allowed that horrific event to happen to get people's attention and get them back in church (and it worked!). But it's no surprise that the numbers declined very quickly after they started saying that. Because the people who had lost, family members and were seeking comfort from this Person Christians say loves them, were also told that He was the one who killed their loved ones so they would come give Him more attention.

It's like if I set your house on fire just so I can come in, play the hero and rescue you. All of your pets died, and you lost your most valuable possessions, but you would be so grateful that I was there to save your life... that is until you find out that I'm the one responsible for killing your pets, destroying your possessions, and endangering your life in the first place. Your gratefulness would quickly wear off and turn to anger.

Although the Bible says that God causes all things to work out for the good of those who love Him (Romans 8:28), that doesn't mean God causes all things.

Can He use cancer to bring somebody back on track? Yes. Does He? I'm certain of it. But it's important for us to remember that cancer is neither designed nor endorsed by Him. Jesus healed sickness, He never prescribed it. He viewed it as a problem that needed a solution, not as the solution to a problem.

The Truth about Mystery

I used to look at death and tragedy with that sense of mystery that so many Christians do. I believed we weren't supposed to know every little detail of why God does or doesn't do things; I believed that way for the majority of my Christian life.

I was one of the people who would tell others who asked questions, "We are little bitty humans! Do we really think all of God could fit into the mind of man?" unaware at the time that *we have the mind of Christ.* (2 Cor. 2:9).

When you check into New Testament scripture and see what it says regarding the realm of mystery, it's actually very surprising (and comforting) to see how much of it is contrary to what we are taught about it in church.

It is often implied that there are some things God is withholding from us until the proper time comes for them to be revealed (if that time ever comes at all). The idea being that if He reveals those things too early it could very well be catastrophic. What if we're not ready?

I do believe that He teaches us life lessons in as big chunks as we can handle. But at the same time, according to scripture, I think the Truth about His will, His nature and His entire being have been completely revealed out in the open. There is nothing regarding *those things* that remain hidden. And He's certainly not purposely hiding those things from us.

This chapter has a list of New Testament scriptures regarding mystery.; we'll get to those in a moment. Please be sure to go and look those verses up for yourself in whatever Bible translation you have available.

One very important thing I want you to notice is how many of them start off by saying that there *were* things hidden for generations, and God *did* work in mysterious ways to *those* people. They couldn't understand or comprehend God or His ways at that time, *but now*, in these days, those things that were hidden from them have been revealed to us.

What is the shift that happened between the people in the Old Covenant (who couldn't understand God's ways) and us in the New Covenant (who can)?

Jesus.

The Revelation of God in Christ

Jesus is the mystery of God revealed. He's the mind of God, the heart of God, the thoughts of God, the will of God, and the ways of God, all revealed, plainly seen and understood (Hebrews 1:3, Colossians 1:15, John 5:19).

When we attempt to understand Christ through our circumstance, we will always find mystery. But when we try to understand our circumstance through Christ, we will always find a revelation of God's heart on the matter.

For example, if I try to understand God through my sickness, I will more than likely come to the conclusion that He has allowed me to have that sickness for some mysterious purpose, because… *hello! Think, McFly!* common sense says that if He didn't want me to have the sickness I wouldn't have it. Sadly that's the conclusion that most people who grow up in church come to whenever they become sick or lose a close loved one to sickness.

If however, I try to understand my sickness through the life of Jesus, I can see very clearly that He never once allowed anybody He encountered to remain sick for any reason whatsoever. And since He is the full revelation of the Father, I can safely conclude that it's not God's will or desire, for me or anybody else to be sick—ever.

New Testament Scriptures about Mystery

Here are some of the verses about the mysteries of God.

Note: I've either kept the commas and semi-colons, or have added an ellipsis as an indication that the verse continues. Yes, I'm openly admitting to purposely quoting some of these verses out of context. It isn't done with the intention of hiding anything from you, but with the intention of keeping you focused on the point. As always, you are highly encouraged to look these verses up in their full context.

Because it has been given to you to know the mysteries of the kingdom of heaven, (Matt. 13:11, NKJV)

To you it has been given to know the mystery of the kingdom of God; (Mark 4:11, NKJV)

The knowledge of the secrets of the Kingdom of God has been given to you, (Luke 8:10, GNT)

I do not call you servants any longer, for the servant does not know what his master is doing (working out). But I have called you My friends, because I have made known to you everything that I have heard from My Father. [I have revealed to you everything that I have learned from Him.] (John 15:15, AMP)

Now to him who is able to establish you in accordance with my gospel, the message I proclaim about Jesus Christ, in keeping with the revelation of the mystery hidden for long ages past, but now revealed and made known through the prophetic writings by the command of the eternal God, so that all the Gentiles might come to the obedience that comes from faith... (Romans 16:25-26, NIV)

No, we declare God's wisdom, a mystery that has been hidden and that God destined for our glory before time began. None of the rulers of this age understood it, for if they had, they would not have crucified the Lord of glory. However, as it is written:

"What no eye has seen, what no ear has heard, and what no human mind has conceived—the things God has prepared for those who love him—

These are the things God has revealed to us by his Spirit. (1 Cor. 2:7-10, NIV)

Who has known the mind of the Lord so as to instruct him?

But we have the mind of Christ. (1 Cor. 2:16, NIV)

the mystery which has been hidden from ages and from generations, but now has been revealed to His saints. To them God has chosen to make known among the Gentiles the glorious riches of this mystery, which is Christ in you, the hope of glory. (Col. 1:26-27, NKJV)

I want them to be encouraged and knit together by strong ties of love. I want them to have complete confidence that they understand God's mysterious plan, which is Christ himself. (Col. 2:2, NLT)

And pray for us, too, that God may open a door for our message, so that we may proclaim the mystery of Christ, for which I am in chains. (Col. 4:3, NIV)

He made known to us the mystery of his will according to his good pleasure, which he purposed in Christ, (Eph. 1:9, NIV)

Surely you have heard about the administration of God's grace that was given to me for you, that is, the mystery made known to me by revelation, as I have already written briefly. (Eph. 3:2-3, NIV)

Also to enlighten all men and make plain to them what is the plan [regarding the Gentiles and providing for the salvation of all men] of the mystery kept hidden through the ages and concealed until now in [the mind of] God Who created all things by Christ Jesus. (Eph. 3:9, AMP)

Can It Be Any Clearer?

What was a mystery to them has been revealed to us in Christ. God, who is light, isn't holding us in the dark about anything. God, who is good, is not withholding any good from us (Psalm 84:11).

The only lack of revelation is on our end in what we fail to perceive about who He is and what He has accomplished for us. God does work in mysterious ways to those who don't know Him, but God worked through Christ, who is the mystery of God revealed.

If you know Christ, you know the revealed mystery of God.

If God works in a way that is mysterious to us, it should be a sign of an area where we do not yet know Him, but it's also an area where we can know him, and where He wants us to.

But I have called you my friends, because I have made known to you everything that I have heard from My Father. (John 15:15, NIV)

Jesus made everything known to the disciples, yet they did not yet understand everything at that time. It wasn't because He was holding out on them or had willingly blinded them to it (He told them the exact opposite), but it was ignorance on their end of who He was and what He came to accomplish. However, later on after Christ rises from the dead, they finally understand the big picture.

In today's church, the biggest source of our lack of answers is our abundant lack of questions. The disciples were full of questions for Jesus, and He was always full of answers right back (often in the form of questions of His own).

If there is anything that is "mysterious" to you about God, ask Him about it and He will tell you. Holy Spirit came to lead us into all (not some) Truth. (John 16:13)

In the next chapter I want to explore a little deeper into asking questions.

The Greatest Secret to Growth

Time after time throughout the year, we hear emotional speeches that sound something like this: "We're going be a generation who will rise up and live pure and holy for the Lord! This people rising up will serve God with their whole heart in absolute freedom, without looking to the left or the right!"

Oftentimes when we hear buzzwords like *generation* or *rising up*, it's almost like we're programmed to know that's our cue—the part where we all lift our arms up and yell things like,

"Amen!"

"Hallelujah!"

"Thank you, Lord!"

Year after year, we get excited about and look forward to those things, but none of the hype is ever lived up to, and none of the promises ever fulfilled. Yet, every year when our great prophets take the stage to say the same exact thing they said the previous year(s), we fall for it all over again.

"Amen!"

"Hallelujah!"

"Thank you, Lord!"

The Recurring Problem

Have you ever noticed how it's always *on the horizon, around the corner*, and *rising up*? And it always seems to stay there while we are constantly made to feel like those things will only change if we try our hardest to change our behavior and be good boys and girls? If we keep the sin out of our lives, remember to repent, confess each and every one of our sins, ask for forgiveness, and most importantly, pay our tithes and offerings, then around the corner will finally become a reality.

But since those things are not yet a reality, you can be sure that it's your fault that God is so reluctant. You're not trying hard enough, and God is not impressed enough by your effort to live holy to send another outpouring of His Spirit and forgive the sin of the nation.

There is always something we have to do, or we're not doing right, or we're not doing enough of. And whenever you try harder and it still isn't working, it's because you *still* aren't trying hard enough or doing enough of... whatever it your leaders are demanding of you.

"You've got to have more faith, brother!"

"Wait on the Lord, brother!"

"Try fasting, brother!"

"Be patient, brother!"

"You can't always be on the mountain top, brother!"

I listened to all of that advice for years. But I finally got to the point where all the stock answers and corny Christian catch-phrases weren't good enough for my problems. Sure, they were good for making me feel better (read: apathetic) about my situation, but I no longer wanted to feel better about my situation, I wanted a *new* situation.

I had been running on the religious hamster wheel for years, and one day I had reached my limit. I was so exhausted from striving to change things, and so disappointed that nothing was ever changing, that I stopped, looked around, and asked God, "Why am I even doing this? What's the point? Because they said I'm supposed to? Why am I supposed to?"

As I lay there in bed after years of striving to win the acceptance of God by trying to fulfill all of my religious duties, in pure frustration I asked God, "What is the point of being a Christian if I have to try my hardest to keep these rules that are impossible to keep? If I'm inevitably going to sin anyway, why don't I just go do whatever I want and get it over with?"

Maybe that was an offensive question to ask Him, maybe not. I didn't care. I was offended at the hopelessness of being expected to keep unkeepable rules.

Truthfully, I didn't even want to live anymore. I often fell asleep asking God to keep me from waking up the next morning, while imagining myself putting a gun in my mouth, or a noose around my neck, or many of the other "get out of jail free" cards.

I fantasized about how much easier it would be if I just didn't have to be stuck doing what I was doing for my entire life, knowing (from the often misinterpreted Romans 7) that it was just "my nature" to do the stuff I hated doing. There's no good news in that.

The Day Everything Changed

In the summer of 2009, my friend and I took a trip to southern California to get an impartation from Paul Cain.

Most of the way there (a seven hour drive) I just vented about all of my problems and perceived shortcomings with my Christian life. "I feel like I'm not doing enough!" I passionately whined, "I should be out healing the sick, and preaching to homeless people, and not sinning so much, and reading my Bible and praying more! I haven't been doing any of that stuff like I should be doing!"

My friend replied gently and said, "The word 'should' died on the cross." Then He asked, "Did you know, in John 15, Jesus compares us to branches?"

"Yeah?" I replied.

"Think about how branches bear fruit," he said as he scrunched up his face, making sure to keep his eyes on the road, "Do they stress, and strive to make fruit grow, and try to work up this feeling of accomplishment? Or do they just rest, and the fruit is produced naturally because they are connected to the tree?"

I listened intently, answering each of his questions silently in my head.

He continued, "Now I know that I could lie in my bed for the rest of my life and do nothing, and God wouldn't love me any more or any less than He does right now. Jesus said, 'It is finished!' What does finished mean? It's done. Nothing we do or don't do can add to or take away from what He already did. We just rest in His accomplishments."

I stayed silent, processing every word and feeling my insides come alive. I imagine it's how Peter felt in John 6 when he told Jesus, "You alone have the words of life," because it felt like every word my friend spoke was adding more life to the deepest part of my spirit. This was the gospel.

He went on to tell me what the new creation verse in 2 Corinthians (5:17) is actually talking about. That we were changed from sinners into saints, and now it was no longer my nature to sin. I could actually choose not to do the things I hated doing.

That was it! The life-changing answer to that question I had asked God so many months before!

Q: What is the point of trying to keep all of these unkeepable rules?

A: That's not the point. The point is to take your eyes off of your own work (the do's and don't's) and put them on Christ's work (the *done*).

It instantly changed my perspective. I could be a happy Christian and enjoy a happy God who loved me for me, not for what I did for Him. I had been a Christian for years, but now I was truly free. I had finally heard the gospel. In contrast, what I called freedom in Christ before felt like being tied to a tree with chains and left for dead, and I was just about there before I heard the message of His grace.

• • •

Permission to Ask Questions

Over the next few months following my newfound life, I began to question everything I heard from the pulpit. All of those questions I had kept repressed for the previous years were free to bounce around in my head, and I felt neither ashamed nor doubtful for having them.

If anybody even hinted about me having to work and strive for what only comes by grace, or if anyone implied that I was just a dirty rotten sinner who was prone to sin, I would happily counter it in my head and say, "No way! Jesus finished it! I get to enjoy that kind of life for free!"

I have found asking questions to be one of the most powerful tools we have. It's a superpower, and one of the most underestimated powers we have—not only in religious circles, but life in general. It is, in my opinion, the single greatest secret to growth.

A person becomes an instant danger to the system when they stop turning the gears and ask, "Why am I doing this?" The world and the religious system both rely on people to be oblivious to the reason behind what they are doing. It provides cliché quotes and hopeful promises, relying on people to think, "This is just the normal life, and everybody works this hard to slowly climb the ladder. Eventually, if I keep my head down and work hard enough, things will get better!"

Movies like, *The Matrix*, *V for Vendetta*, *Braveheart*, *Equilibrium*, *The Bourne Trilogy* and countless others are based on a premise of people being controlled by an authority that has been in place for years; so many years, in fact, that blindly going along with whatever that system demands is considered "normal." Not going along with it is rebellious and brings consequence. But the protagonist inevitably gets to a point where he has to ask (in one way or another) "Why?" and then he decides not to do things the "normal" way anymore. He challenges the authority of the system that had kept his people oppressed for years, and of course, the system tries to destroy him for his disloyalty. Many of his closest allies soon mark him as an enemy and withdraw relationship.

Every reformation starts with a question, "Why do we have to do things their way?" And then a decision to do things a different way. Of course, the choice to revolt often results in war, because if the system were to just let people live outside of its boundaries, it would no longer be able to survive. The people inside its boundaries are the ones turning the gears that are keeping it alive. If all of those people were to suddenly *wake up* and realize what they've been doing, the system immediately ceases to function.

You have permission to ask questions. You have permission to quit turning the gears of religion in blind obedience to your leaders, and demand answers from them just as they demand labor from you.

You Don't Need Blind Faith to be Faithful

One of the best things I've ever learned is that God is not offended by my questions. Where other people will say, "You just need to have more faith," or "Who are you to question God?" or "His ways are higher than yours," or "God doesn't owe you an explanation," and where they will try to make you feel ashamed and inferior for daring to question why or how God does things, God himself has never done that to me.

Never.

Not even once.

I used to think that's how He was towards me because the only reference point I had for His character was the other Christians around me. So they were easily able to convince me that I shouldn't ask question and I should just have faith (and somehow we think those things are at odds with each other). Yet, wasn't it Him who said, "Ask, and you will receive"? He didn't say, "Ask, and I will respond with condescending tone, telling you why it's out of line for you to question me!"

Ask the question, receive the answer; don't ask the question, don't receive the answer.

Encouraging blind obedience ("You don't need a reason to do it, just do it!") while discouraging questions ("Just shut up and have faith!") is a manipulation tactic used by tyrants and cult leaders. It's a form of brainwashing. It's how they keep people under their control, by making you feel faithless and doubtful towards something you value highly (like your country or your God) for even daring to think about questioning how the leader is doing things. They compare doubt towards your leaders to having doubt towards your country, your God, or disloyalty to the group of people you've placed your life on the line to protect.

(One example is that whenever I talk about how I quit attending church. It's almost guaranteed that somebody will come along with the "do not forsake the fellowship" Bible verse as a way to imply that, because I don't attend a Church service, I am automatically abandoning the Church and all of my Christian brothers. Unfortunately for them (and fortunately for me), I recognize the manipulation there, so it doesn't dictate my behavior by making me feel guilty for not attending church services.)

See, if the tyrants and cult leaders can get you to stop thinking with your own mind (by suppressing your desire to ask questions), then there is no other alternative than for you to start thinking with their mind (by accepting their exact ideals and beliefs about every situation).

However, if they cannot get you under control, and you continue to question their cause, they either kill you or lock you up for treason. It has happened all throughout history, and whether you're aware of it or not, those same bully tactics are used throughout the church today by some of the most well respected church leaders in our country. Except instead of murdering you physically or locking you in prison, they just kick you out of their churches and murder your reputation in front of all their followers.

If you look around, that's why so many Christians today sound like exact replicas of their favorite preachers and prophets, while parroting everything they say and do. They've quit asking questions and have just accepted that their leader is right about everything, and "don't touch the Lord's anointed." Don't question, just submit to your spiritual leaders (regardless of where they are leading you).

I'm not at all implying that this manipulation is always intentional (I choose to trust Jesus when He said "they know not what do"), neither am I saying that all pastors are tyrants or cult leaders. What I'm saying is that when you take away a person's ability to ask questions (which is done in the church by making people feel faithless towards God and disloyal to their peers), you take away their ability to be the individual genius they are; and soon they begin mindlessly replicating their glorious leader.

Since they don't know who they are, being themselves is not an option, but since they have become so familiar with the traits and characteristics of their leader, they can act like, him/her easily.

We have this idea that questioning what God does and why He does it is a sign of doubt towards Him. That's ridiculous. When children ask a thousand questions, is it because they are doubtful of your parenting skills, or because they have a genuine desire to learn how and why you do things?

If we don't ask questions, we won't have answers; if we don't have answers, we won't have change. Never let anyone diminish the power of a question, make your demand for answers seem childish and unimportant, or distort what is your genuine desire to learn by making you feel ashamed and embarrassed for asking questions (and trust me, they will try).

It's not a parable when scripture says, *test everything and hold on to what is good* (1 Thess. 5:21). But what happens if you don't test anything? You will hold on to *everything*, whether it's good or bad.

Some people will try to make you look and feel silly for being full of questions, implying that you're full of doubt. Others will boldly declare, "We aren't supposed to have all the answers!" in a desperate attempt to get you to remain as naive about reality as they are, thinking it's as normal to live in the dark as they do. Don't let yourself be shaken by them. Those who ask the life-changing questions will find the life-changing answers, and those with the life-changing answers will change the world.

Does that mean I have all of the answers? *Ha!* Not even close! But with every question I ask, I come one step closer to having another answer that has the potential to change my life and the lives of others I encounter.

If for some reason I were only allowed to give one word of advice in my entire lifetime, it would be to ask the hardest questions you can think of, and ask them often. Even if you're not asking other people, ask yourself, and ask

Holy Spirit. He was sent to lead us into all Truth. He loves to answer our questions. He loves to teach us. We only have to remain teachable so we can hear Him when He teaches.

Have you ever noticed how often the disciples asked Jesus to explain a parable? Or even, "Why couldn't we heal the sick boy?" Asking questions is your right, not only as a Christian towards your pastor, but as a son towards your Father.

A Look at Popular Traditions

Many of our popular church traditions don't allow us to be teachable because we already have some kind of slick sounding answer for everything. Although most of those answers aren't even in scripture, we settle for them every time because they came from behind a pulpit. There comes a day when it just isn't enough anymore.

When the disciples prayed for the sick boy and he didn't get healed, they went to Jesus to find out why, and He told them. Yet, when people today pray for the sick boy and He doesn't get healed, we don't ask Jesus why, we just agree with the pastor who boldly declares at the boy's funeral, "This was God's will!'" And everybody says? "Amen!" (Which unfortunately means "so be it.")

Let's take a look at few of the common answers we've come up with over the years.

Q: "Why am I going through a hard time?"

A: "God must be trying to teach you a lesson so He can stretch your faith! Look at Job!"

Q: "Why hasn't God healed my mom's cancer?"

A: "God must be trying to get her attention so she'll go back to church!"

Q: "Why did God allow that cancer to kill my mom?"

A: "God must have wanted her in heaven so she wouldn't suffer here on earth!"

In our churches today, we don't need Him for answers because we've already created our own, put them on magnets and bumper stickers, and given Him credit for the quote because we heard it from a pulpit, where the man claims to be speaking a word from the Lord. And once we accept that it's a word from the Lord, we make it impossible to disagree with. To disagree with "a word from the Lord" is to disagree with the Lord Himself and no Christian in their right mind would ever want to get caught doing that.

You will never find Jesus giving any one of the above answers to anyone. The only reason we accept those answers is because they've been hammered into our heads for so long by our leaders that they've become normal. They're the only answers much of the western church has ever given us for our tragic situations; unfortunately, they're often the only answers the western church has.

Eventually, however, you begin to ask different questions, and inevitably find different answers.

If you ask the questions everyone else is afraid to, you will get the answers that none of them have. It doesn't take a special anointing, just a willingness to be uncompromising in your pursuit of truth.

Here are some of the questions I began to ask in response to the many of the popular answers I've received in church:

Q: Where did Jesus ever give someone sickness to stretch their faith?

A: Nowhere. He didn't give or allow sickness; He healed every single person who came to Him (Acts 10:38).

Q: Where did Jesus ever give someone sickness to get them to worship Him?

A: Nowhere. He healed them for their benefit, not His own (*Love is not self-seeking*).

Q: Where did Jesus ever allow sickness to kill someone so they could go to heaven where that sickness wouldn't kill them?

A: Nowhere. He didn't want anybody to suffer from sickness on earth, so He healed them on earth; every single one (Acts 10:38).

When you bring everything back to Jesus, those types of answers are simple to find.

But to be upfront with you, although I believe it's God's will to heal every single person and fix every single problem on this planet, I haven't seen every person I've prayed for healed.

Right now as I write this, I have a lazy eye I've had since I was born, a lisp I've had since I could talk, a chipped tooth that I broke a few months ago (on a Cheeto of all things), and my eye sight has become significantly worse over the past year. Have I prayed for those things? Countless times; still not much change. That's one major "Why's" I don't yet have an answer for, but I'll talk more about how to deal with those kinds of disappointments in the next chapter.

The Faith of a Child

Christians are famous for telling people to be "child-like" and yet one of the greatest qualities of a child (the never ending list of questions) is often discouraged.

It's often said that between the ages of two and five are the most important years of a child's growth. What do they annoy us with the most during that short period of time? Nonstop questions, of course!

We often get frustrated and say, "Oh my goodness, you ask too many questions!" and we send them away. However, the best thing we can do for them is encourage and invite them to ask even more questions so they can grow as much as they can in that small window of time.

If they are asking those questions because they are in the process of growing, what does that say to me? That asking questions is a vital key to rapid growth. Nobody teaches a child to ask questions, they are taught *out* of it by adults. They naturally seek knowledge so they can grow; they have to be taught not to.

It's not uncommon that in a church system we would just toss someone in parking lot ministry, or make them an usher and tell them it will be a good place for them to grow. I disagree. While they will gain experience as an usher or as a minister of parking lots, if you really want them in a good place to grow then put them in an environment where they can be curious without boundaries and ask questions without limitations (including the offensive, religiously-incorrect kinds of questions).

"But what if we don't have answers?"

I think that's the common fear among leaders, and oftentimes the reason questions are discouraged and people are sent away. Nobody wants to be the one to say "I don't know." But if you don't have the answer to a question, it's better to say, "I don't know, but I'll help you find it," than it is to just start making things up for the sake of upholding a certain image, or just sending someone away and making them feel like they are doing something wrong for asking.

If you're a leader, you at least want to lead people in the right direction, don't you?

Look at the Signs

Have you ever been walking down the street and someone pulls over and says something like, "Hey, I'm lost, do you know how to get to the freeway from here?" We probably all have cars by now and don't deal with that much, but I used to walk to the store a lot and that would happen to me occasionally. Whenever it did I wouldn't just point in a random direction and say, "That way! Go that way!" If I knew the answer, I would say, "Yes, it's right up the hill, make a left turn and it will be on your immediate right, you can't miss it!" Or else I would say, "Sorry, I really don't know. But I can pull up a map on my phone and find it."

In the latter case, it's really amazing, because at first you didn't know, but now, because you helped another person find the answer to their question, you also have the answer for yourself. Best of all, you didn't just make something up and potentially get that person more lost than they already were.

This is in no way a command, but it's my opinion that we should never discourage anyone from asking questions, and we should try to answer as many questions as we can, or at least point them in the right direction. And please, if you don't have the answers right then, don't give them some cop-out excuse like, "We're not meant to know the answer to that." Jesus never did that.

Imagine that in the context of the freeway example.

"Hey, can you help me? I don't know how to get to the freeway from here."

"Yeah, neither do I! That's just one of many mysteries of life! We aren't meant to know the answer to that until we get to heaven!"

I'm completely ignoring the fact that there are large green signs everywhere that point directly towards the freeway.

The issue isn't that it's something we aren't meant to know, it's that it's something I don't know, and I've become too apathetic about the problem to look for a solution. If you would acknowledge the big green signs that say, "Freeway Entrance, turn left!" you would have the answer to the "mystery" that might otherwise avoid you until you reach the pearly gates.

When you help people find the answer (and even help them come up with more questions), not only will they grow, but you will grow with them. And through that a relationship between the two of you is guaranteed to become stronger and stronger. You're figuring life out together, which is what relationship is.

Can the onslaught of questions be annoying? Oh my goodness, you bet! Even after writing this chapter and reading it dozens of times during rewrites, I was still finding myself annoyed whenever my 5-year-old niece would barge into my room asking a million questions. (*Come on, I'm trying to write a book about asking questions! Quit asking so many questions!*) But annoyance, in my opinion, is actually only a fruit of self-centeredness, and it's supposed to be about them growing and learning, not about us being inconvenienced by their desire to.

I'm well aware that there are times when we really are too busy to sit down and answer a million questions. In times like that, it may be a good idea to have them write down those questions so they don't forget, and then you can discuss them later. In writing those questions down, they may even figure out the answer for themselves before you get back to them (then they can teach you what they've learned!).

Remain Teachable

It's important to remain teachable because you never know when you're going to be taught (unless you only schedule a two-hour-window for it on Sunday mornings). You never know when the answer to that thing you've been wondering will suddenly pop into your mind.

Always be ready to learn, but always question what you learn and see if it measures up to scripture, and more importantly, the person of Jesus (more on that in the next chapter).

When you stop bringing everything back to religious quotes, feel good catch-phrases, and your undying commitment to your pastor, and when you stop settling for those religious cop-out answers and you start bringing everything back to the accomplishments of the cross and the person of Jesus, you will quickly find the answers to those nagging questions that everyone else pressures you to sweep under the carpet and forget about.

I'll tell you straightaway that those answers will more often than not go against what your pastor so passionately preached in his sermon last Sunday. It's nothing personal against him, but wrong is wrong, and for the sake of moving forward that old stuff must be rejected, and if given the privilege by the person, corrected.

It doesn't matter whether that wrong is said in an outburst of anger and slip of the tongue, or if that wrong was the result of a week's worth of passion, prayer, and research to prepare a Sunday sermon. If wrong is not dealt with and continues to be promoted as right, it will perpetually produce bad fruit under the guise of a good tree—I don't think I have to point out how dangerous that is.

Those doctrines quickly become a wolf in sheep's clothing, which never ends well for the other sheep in the pen.

Correcting Doctrines

Notice that I say doctrines, not people. The target isn't people, and the goal isn't to correct wrong doctrines merely for the sake of correcting wrong doctrines. It's important to remember that just because somebody is teaching something you disagree with (even if they are factually wrong), that doesn't mean they are your enemy.

As much as doctrines are important in Christianity, when we value them in a way that makes it okay for us to mistreat other people, we've missed the entire point.

It's easy to get caught up on trivial issues about right and wrong doctrine. That's not the kind of right and wrong I'm referring to here. I define "wrong" by what hurts people, not by how different their opinions are from my own.

It hasn't always been that way. I've spent countless hours arguing with people just because they had different perspectives than I did about the same verse and the goal was to show them how right I was. I learned the hard way that that's a very frustrating way to live.

Now I judge right and wrong by whether or not something hurts more people than it helps. If it's making a 23-year-old lay in bed at night wishing they were dead, then yes, that's a doctrine I'm going to counter, correct and demolish without shame or remorse, because it's threatening a person's life.

If a doctrine is just making people call God by different names than I do, or causing them to call Saturday the *real* Sabbath day, why should that be of any concern to me? It has no effect on a person's well-being.

You Have the Answers

I no longer call you servants, because servants don't know what their master is doing. But now I call you friends, because I have told you everything that my Father told me. (John 15:15)

He's always had the answers, we've just never been taught to go to Him for them, even though we proudly do that *Christian thing* where we declare Jesus as our answer.

I used to do that a lot, but for being so confident that I know Jesus, and Jesus is my answer, it's amazing how many answers I didn't have. If He's your answer but you still don't have answers, He is either keeping you in the dark, or you're just not being honest with yourself about who you're letting influence your life. You are valuing the words of your pastors over the words of Jesus.

Am I saying that because you know Jesus, you should automatically know the answers to every problem, and if you don't there is something wrong with you? Not at all! Please don't take it that way, and please don't let any shameful feelings creep in if you're now thinking of questions you don't yet have answers to.

As mentioned earlier, I still don't have all of the answers, and I may very well leave this planet without all of them. I don't think it's realistic to gain all of the answers myself either. If that were the case, I wouldn't need to be part of a Body. My hand has answers to problems that my feet don't, and vice versa. They do different things and have different functions… we know the analogy.

I may never have answers for how to end world hunger because I'm not going in that direction, neither have I pursued the answers to that question. But I know God is not keeping the answer to that question hidden from us for some great and mysterious reason. If He were, that would make Him responsible for the problem. And if He's responsible for the problem, that "God is good" thing we always quote goes straight out the window.

The answer is there, but somebody has to hear it before they can act on it, and more importantly, before they can hear the answer, they first have to ask the question.

If you don't know everything, that's fine. If you don't know how to get to the freeway from here, that's fine. But don't live in such a way that makes it seem as if our Father is the one keeping those things from us for some intentionally mysterious purpose while people suffer and die because of it.

It was Him who said, *My people perish for lack of knowledge.* Will we then accuse Him of withholding that knowledge from us, and consequently accuse Him of being solely responsible for those who perish? Aren't we the very same ones trying to convince the world that He is good, and that He loves them?

The Most Common Reason for Lack of Answers

The reason I believe so many people don't have answers is because they are basing their life on everyone in scripture except Christ (who is the answer to every question), or they are taking their pastor's word about everything and not double-checking. It often sounds like this:

If I lose a loved one: "Look what happened to Job! The Lord gives and takes away!"

If I want to end abortion and bring revival: "Look at the persistent widow in Luke 18! We must cry out to God like the woman cried out to the unjust judge!" (The implication being that God is like an unjust judge who's very reluctant about bringing justice.)

If I want Jesus to return: "Look at John the Baptist! I must prepare the way for the Lord! He must increase, I must decrease!"

But how often do we hear, "Look at Christ and what He did!"?

In that case, if I lose a loved one, I say, "Look at Christ. He never tolerated sickness or death. This wasn't His will!"

If I want to end abortion and bring revival: "Look at Christ. He brought revival everywhere He went and held no one's sin against them. He sent me to do the same!" (John 20:21)

If I want Jesus to return: "Christ lives in me! Where I go, He goes!"

We are **Christ**ians—followers of **Christ** and His life, nobody else.

Contrary to what gets pumped into our minds all around this country, this isn't an "Elijah Generation," or an

"Esther Generation," this is a Jesus generation. It has been, and always will be all about Jesus.

Here is a very simple and trustworthy saying that deserves full acceptance: If it's not about Christ, it's not Christianity.

In the final chapter of this book, I want to show you a practical way to rightly divide the word.

Right and Wrong & the Measuring Rod of Truth

As I've said time and time again throughout this book, many of the popular doctrines in the church today don't actually have much (if anything) to do with Jesus. They're more based on personal experiences and disappointments than anything else.

I've also quoted 1 Thess. 5:21 numerous times, *test everything and hold on to the good* (It's one of my favorite verses in the Bible, after all!), but I obviously want to show you how to actually do that.

Before you test anything at all, you first have to have something to test it up against. As the classic example goes, you can't spot a counterfeit $20 bill if you don't know what a genuine $20 bill looks like... unless you have one of those magic markers that automatically tells you if one is counterfeit or not.

In this chapter, I hope to provide you with one of those markers.

The common Christian belief would be that you want to test everything next to the Bible to see if it's right about God. However, that's not always the best idea.

Wait! Don't slam the book down just yet! Let me explain.

Not Everything You Hear about God is True about God

While I believe the Bible is true, I don't believe everything in the Bible is true about God. I won't go too deep into that here, as it could probably take up an entire book in itself, but I'll give you a general idea of what I'm talking about.

Try this: next time you're out in public pay attention to someone's shadow. It doesn't matter who, just pick someone. Without studying the person, study their shadow for about ten seconds or so. Then see how much you can figure out about that person, merely based on the information you've gathered from their shadow.

Can you tell how tall they are? How about their ethnicity? How about their tone of voice? Can you tell what color eyes they have? Can you see if they are smiling or frowning? How about their age? Are they optimistic or pessimistic? Are they easily angered or quick to forgive?

You probably can't come to an accurate conclusion about any of those things just from looking at their shadow. A shadow is merely a silhouette; a darkened outline of what they actually look like. The reality of who that person is (height, weight, eye color, smile, frown, age, ethnicity, etc.) can only be seen in the physical body of the person. In order to go even deeper and find out personality traits, like whether they are optimistic or pessimistic, or easily angered or quick to forgive, you would actually have to talk to them and form a relationship.

What's the point?

Jesus said, *no one knows the Father except the Son...* (Matt. 11:27). Paul said the old covenant of the law was a shadow of the good things to come, the reality of those good things, however, is found in Christ (Col. 2:17, Heb. 10:1).

When reading the Old Testament descriptions of God, you have to understand that those people were only looking at a shadow. They didn't know God like those of us under the New Covenant. They were only seeing a darkened image of God—a silhouette. So while there are indeed plenty of true descriptions of God in the Old Testament (I've used some in this book), not every description is true.

So do you just throw the Old Testament out and conclude that it's deceptive and misleading about God? Do you just pick and choose the verses that make you feel good and agree with your opinions, and disregard the ones that don't? No, you just figure out how to distinguish between what's true about God and what isn't.

How do you do that? You quit looking at the shadow and you look at the person, the reality, Jesus. Although Jesus said *no one has seen the Father except the Son*, He also said *if you have seen me you have seen the Father*. Paul went on to say in Col. 1:15 and Hebrews 1:3 that Jesus is the exact representation of God's being (character, nature, etc.). He is the visible image of the invisible God.

What does that all mean? It means if you want the most accurate representation of God and what He looks like (in character, virtue, personality, etc.), you don't look at the Psalms, or the book of Isaiah, or the story of Job, you look at Jesus.

Believe Everything I Tell You!

Unfortunately that doesn't often happen. Instead, as I've said throughout the book, many people just take their favorite pastor's/prophet's/apostle's/author's word for everything, or read the descriptions their favorite Bible characters give about God and make their lives revolve around that.

They read what David wrote about God in his moments of despair and frustration and conclude that, just because it's in the Bible, it must automatically be an accurate description of how God is. Then they read the descriptions David gave when he wasn't in despair and frustration and it's the exact opposite of the God he was talking about elsewhere. So we look at two contrary descriptions of God and conclude that both ideas are right about Him. One minute we say "God loves the world unconditionally," and the next, "If America doesn't keep God's laws (i.e. His *conditions*), He's going to destroy it for its sin!" (in love, of course!)

We've spiritualized those kinds of contradictions so much, and have made so many excuses for them that it's not really a big deal to us. Yes, *for God so loved the world that He sent His son...* But God also so hates sin that He doesn't mind killing the sinner. After all, "God is love, but He is also just!" Translation: "God is Jekyll, but He is also Hyde."

Much of the problem is that position in the church is often valued over Truth; meaning anyone in a position of religious authority can lead the people wherever they please without much (if any) resistance.

"You're a pastor? Okay, I can trust what you tell me about God!"

"You're a popular Bible character? You DEFINITELY know what you're talking about!"

"You're a Christian author who published a book? You must have a clue!"

"You're a popular and well-respected worship leader with a bunch of hit songs? The lyrics you write must be so accurate!"

It's quite obvious that the vast majority of Christians don't actually know how to compare what they hear from the pulpit about God, with who God really is in the Bible. I don't say that as if I'm superior to those people, or all-knowing. In fact, most of my Christian life so far was spent that same way, so I can empathize.

For years I just believed whatever I was told about God because the only frame of reference I had for what kind of person He is was other people's interpretation and understanding of scripture.

But there are so many different interpretations and understandings of God and scripture nowadays that if you don't know how to interpret scripture and learn to understand God on your own (without anybody else's filter), you're likely to just pick a favorite leader and idolize them.

Soon your God begins to look more like a Bill Johnson, John Piper, Mark Driscoll, or Misty Edwards, than He does Jesus. And since you receive your identity from their idea of God, any idea of God that's opposed to theirs is automatically seen as (and treated like) heresy. And the person proposing that idea is often treated like an enemy (except not the way Jesus said to treat your enemies).

Building Your House

Let's say I'm building a new door for my house. Before I start building the door I have to know how tall and how wide the door frame is. If I just build the door without taking those things into consideration, the odds of me getting it to fit aren't very good. It might come out too short, too wide, or any number of problems.

Getting the exact measurements of the door frame is *vital*.

My good friend, Ryan, just so happens to be at my house helping me out; he looks at the door frame and says, "Hm. I would say the door frame is 5 feet, 9 inches tall, and 6 feet, 1 inches wide." Okay, thanks Ryan. Those sound like they would be the correct measurements to something.

Now, here's the all-important question: should I take Ryan's word for it and start building the door according to the measurements he has given me? Or should I double check for myself, just to make sure?

Ryan has said a lot of helpful things in the past, and I trust him because he's my friend. However, it's probably not the best idea to just go along with his guess, is it? I should double check for myself just to be safe.

So how do I check? I grab a tape measure, of course!

A tape measure is designed specifically for getting exact measurements of length and width, meaning I can trust it to be more accurate than an estimate from a friend.

Ryan holds one end to the top of the door frame and I stretch the other end to the floor; 6 feet, 9 inches tall. Ryan then holds one end to the left side of the door frame as I stretch the other end to the right side; 3 feet, 6 inches wide—perfect. I write the numbers down in my notebook so I'll have the information for later.

Now I can base my door on the proper measurements, instead of a quick guess from a friend that would have left the door looking a tad bit too short, and way too wide.

Should Ryan feel bad about guessing wrong? No. It's not that big of a deal and we ended up with the right measurements anyway. But I'm also not going to say, "It's okay, Ryan. You were right in your own way," because he wasn't; and he probably doesn't expect me to say that he was.

According to the instrument designed for measuring length and width, he was pretty far off. However, we can both come together in agreement on the accurate length and width after we look at the results of the measuring tape.

The measuring tape is our basis for truth when measuring the length and width of an object.

Debating Measurements

Now maybe Ryan wants to debate the results of my measurements and measure it himself, and that's okay because the measurements are still based on the truth of the measuring tape.

If done correctly, he should get the same results that I did (or perhaps he'll get different results and we'll find out I'm the one who messed up). However, if he just wants to throw the measuring tape out and say, "I've guessed right in the past, I know I'm right this time," then we will have a problem because we no longer have a solid basis for finding absolute truth.

Truth has been reduced to a matter of opinion and past experience, which makes it a free-for-all because everyone has their own unique opinions and past experiences.

Measuring the Truth about God is honestly just as easy as stretching a tape measure across a doorway. You just need a basis for truth: something that was designed to give accurate results.

Discerning Right and Wrong

As I mentioned earlier in this book, I'm not very big into arguing about right and wrong anymore. Most of my Christian life was spent doing that and it did nothing but leave me frustrated about all of the people who wouldn't agree with me about being right.

However, I do still recognize that it's necessary to be able to discern between what's right and wrong. I don't deny the fact that there are some wrongs that have the potential to destroy a person's entire life (there are also some wrongs that don't).

Here's an example of one that does: I say, "It's always God's will to heal everybody," and somebody's inevitable response will be, "I disagree because I've prayed for many sick people. We prayed for my grandpa and he still died.

We all believed, and it still didn't happen, so it clearly wasn't God's will!"

I've heard responses like that a lot, so let me just be very clear with you: every dead person I've ever prayed for has stayed dead; most of the sick people I've prayed for have stayed sick (some, including my dad, died shortly afterwards).

Do those things hurt? You bet. Are they disappointing? They sure are. Despite what I believe about God's will to heal, losing my dad crushed me. So I can empathize with loss. I can empathize with tragedy. But the question is this: do I rewrite the numbers on the tape measure to fit my experience, or do I continue to trust that the tape measure is always accurate, even when things don't seem right from my own perspective?

I could very well make myself or Ryan feel better about measuring a doorway by rewriting the numbers to match our perspectives, just to say, "See everyone, it wasn't me who got it wrong, it was the tape measure!" But in the long run that will negatively impact anyone else who picks up that tape measure and tries to measure something with it. They will always get inaccurate results of the truth because the object they are using to measure truth is now based on a lie.

If I allow loss and tragedy to cause me to tell other people, in spite of what Jesus says about God, that it's not always His will to heal, then I create a doctrine that gets millions of people to walk around telling the world that God is good, but it's not always His desire to help people.

We might be able to spiritualize those ideas enough to get Christians to believe them ("a spoon full of sugar makes the medicine go down"), but for those who don't yet know Jesus, and are already very cautious of any ideas of God, to them those types of ideas only convince them that they are better off without Him.

When you get pastors at funerals telling their entire congregations that it's God who let that person die, God who gave them that disease, God who decided He would rather let them die a painful death than to heal them, while many Christians won't hesitate to offer their applause and hallelujahs to such statements, people who haven't been indoctrinated by church politics for their entire life hear that and conclude that the God we believe in sounds more like the devil. So it's obvious why they would want nothing to do with Him.

If God's will was for us to get sick, die, and go to heaven, why did He bother putting us on earth?

That's one of the more extreme examples I've encountered in the past few years, but it's one of the ones that actually kills people.

Opinions vs. Facts

We all have our own interpretations of scripture, and a lot of the times that's not as big of a deal as we make it. It's easy to get distracted and only judge right and wrong by who agrees with our personal interpretations of the Bible and who doesn't.

We can often get self-centered about that sort of thing. But that's not the kind of right and wrong I'm referring to here, and it's important to learn to distinguish between facts and opinions (and contrary to what you might believe, strong opinions are not the equivalent of solid facts).

Many look at *facts* and conclude, "It's not a big deal if you see it one way, and somebody else sees it the exact opposite. You're both right!" But that defeats the entire purpose of scripture, which is to be a resource of truth regarding *facts* about God and creation.

There may be many lessons in one story, many applications to one verse, and certainly many unique perspectives (and those things are all okay), but there is no "many ways to be right" when two people believe the exact opposite thing about one subject.

Somebody is right, and somebody is wrong.

In order to find out who's right and who's wrong, there first has to be a basis for finding that absolute, unbiased and unfiltered Truth. Otherwise, as mentioned before, it's just a free-for-all and we should no longer even discuss scripture because anything goes and everyone is right. What is called "one inch" on the tape measure by one person might be called "one foot" by another, and both are right. What's the outcome? Confusion and division; soon our houses start to look very disproportionate.

When the measuring tape is not the basis for truth, people are automatically divided as a result of putting their trust in different people's opinions of that truth. It's what happens when people value teachers above the Teacher Himself.

The Origin of Denominationalism

If Paul was right when He said Christ is the glue that holds all things together (Col. 2), then what happens when you take Christ from the equation? All things fall apart. There is no unity, only division.

How do we think so many different denominations came into existence? (33,000+ to be more specific.) They all trace back to a certain individual's personal perspective of Truth.

"Martin Luther makes a great point about repentance; I will follow him!"

"John Calvin makes a great point about salvation; I will follow him!"

"Bill Johnson makes a great point about healing; I will follow him!"

"Lou Engle makes a great point about intercession; I will follow him."

And so those people who look up to great leaders create entire doctrines and denominations that are based around their teachings, forgetting all about the Person Christianity is all about.

The result is as I mentioned in another chapter, that because people don't know how to find truth for themselves, they soon find themselves following and valuing the teachings of truth according to other people, which leaves them very vulnerable to deception.

Some of you are saying, "I am a follower of Paul." Others are saying, "I follow Apollos." or "I follow Peter," or "I follow only Christ." Can Christ be divided into pieces? Was I, Paul, crucified for you? Were any of you baptized into the name of Paul? (1 Cor. 1:12, NLT)

Even there, it's obvious that Paul is saying, "Take your eyes off of me! I didn't do anything for you! Christ is the main focus here!" Paul was only there to preach the truth according to Christ, not the truth according to Paul, Apollos, Peter, John the Baptist, Elijah, Charles Spurgeon, or Lou Engle.

It was, and only is about Christ.

Discerning the Truth

According to popular Calvinist teachers, the book of Job blatantly proves that God allows the devil to steal, kill, and destroy, all for the purpose of bringing Him glory and emphasizing His supremacy.

Indeed, because of those kinds of interpretations, millions have come to the conclusion that the Father of Lights is in cahoots with the Prince of Darkness (Q: *What fellowship can light have with darkness?*). However, looking at the life of Jesus, my conclusion comes out quite different.

Jesus never once allowed the devil to steal, kill, or destroy. In fact, it says the reason He came was to destroy the devil's work (1 John 3:9) and to restore what was lost. He came to put the devil out of business, not to give him a growing list of clients. The miracles, signs and wonders, were, and still are, the demonstration of God's heart for the people: "Be whole!"

If God gave the devil permission to steal, he wouldn't be called a thief.

So who do I believe? The God in Job who seemingly told the devil to destroy, or the God in Jesus who destroyed every work of the devil He encountered? It may seem like a "tension" to some, maybe a contradiction to others, but the answer is simple and it's always the same: **Jesus**.

Even when it appears as if God has gone madman crazy and passionate pastors like John Piper are telling the world that God is the decisive cause of 100,000+ deaths in an earthquake, Jesus is the ultimate and final answer to the questions and misunderstandings we have about the Father.

He is the revelation in the moment of mystery because He perfectly represented the Father's heart for all of us to see clearly.

If you have seen me, you have seen the Father. (John 14:9)

In other words, if there is anything that doesn't resemble the Son, I can confidently conclude that it's not the Father.

"I hear what you're saying. But my pastor preached a great word last week that proved, without a doubt, that God won't heal you if you have unforgiveness in your heart!"

That's very commonly taught, and many people believe it. But instead of automatically buying into it, solely based on the fact that your pastor said it, ask yourself:

Q: "Where did Jesus ever say that to anyone?"

A: _____

Okay, then what's the conclusion? The conclusion is always the same: *The Son is how the Father behaves towards people.*

Your pastor can chain together as many pieces of scripture as he wants to try and show that God won't heal if you have unforgiveness in your heart, or that God is responsible for who dies and who doesn't, but unless Jesus demonstrated that kind of behavior, there's no real basis to believe it. You are merely going along with the numbers somebody else wrote on the measuring tape to make themselves feel better about their disappointments.

The Truth Himself

Jesus, arrogant as He would be called today, self-proclaimed Himself to be The Truth. In doing so He instantly made Himself the measuring tape to which everything else must line up.

If you're not a Christian, you can get away with not believing that as much as I can get away with not following Mohammad because I don't claim to be Muslim. If you are a Christian, however, Jesus is to be that measuring tape. If it doesn't line up with Him, it's automatically classified as a lie—period. No way around it. You can whine about it all you want, but that's the way it is.

People say, "You're arrogant to say you're absolutely right, how can you make such a claim?" Well, in this case, that's how, because the measuring tape I'm using says, "Whatever lines up with me is Truth, whatever doesn't, is not."

Need proof?

Christ is the visible image of the invisible God. (Col. 1:15, NLT)

The Son is the radiance of God's glory, and the exact representation of his being. (Heb. 1:3, NIV)

Everything true about Jesus is true about the Father. Everything Jesus does in a situation is everything the Father would do in that same situation. He said, *I only do what I see my Father doing.*

Is it God's will to heal? Well, what did Jesus do? He healed the sick.

Is it God's will to heal everyone? Well, how many people did Jesus heal? Everyone (Acts 10:38).

Is it God's will that people lose loved ones? Did Jesus ever encounter a dead person and say, "I'd love to bring them back to you, but it's just not my will"?

Jesus makes it easy to distinguish between what's right and wrong about God. You just have to actually look at Him, and stop looking at everyone else.

No More Confusion about God

Now when a well-respected church leader gets behind a pulpit and says, "That storm that just killed 12,000 people was sent by God to teach us a lesson for our sin," and millions of Christians flip on the panic switch and rush into church buildings to beg God to forgive the sins of our nation and spare them from the rod of His wrath, I simply open up my Bible and look at the measuring tape — Jesus.

Did He cause storms or calm them? Did He forgive sins or hold them against people? Well, there you go. Everybody knows He calmed storms. Everybody knows He went around forgiving sins, not holding them against people (2 Cor. 5:19).

So right away, no matter how popular and well-respected a person is, whether they've been doing this for three years or five decades, whether they have one degree or twelve, own a church or a TV station, are my best friend or my favorite pastor, if they try to convince me that God is judging America for its sin (or anything else that paints Him in bad light), they are automatically wrong about who He is. What they are saying doesn't line up with the measuring rod of Truth and what He did. *I have not come to judge the world, but to save it.* (John 12:47).

If I build my life around the numbers somebody else rewrote on the tape measure, then my life will end up distorted because it's now based on a lie. The dimensions of my house will turn out very disproportionate.

Why Correct?

People have often asked me, "Why do you pick on people so much? You're always pointing out problems!" And although I don't consider it picking on *people*, it's true that I do often point out the problems I see in the Christian religious system.

Saying someone is wrong is never to make them feel bad, stupid, or inadequate. Especially taking into consideration that I'm very open about letting people know I used to believe those same things. The only reasons I'm pointing anything out about it is because those things brought a lot of unneeded stress, depression, and anxiety into my life.

The Bible says that all scripture is useful for teaching and correcting. When it corrects you, it's letting you know you're wrong about something you believe. That's not with the intention or tone of being condescending, unloving, divisive, nit-picky or negative, it's solely for the purpose of helping you move forward, and empowering you to live a less exhausting life.

Most of Paul's letters were written to correct churches that were steeped in life-damaging errors. Throughout every letter he is never shaming them, but instead reassuring them of how much he loves them. Yet, he was still correcting them and saying, *Listen up, what you're doing over here is amazing, I love it! You're so gifted and passionate! I brag to all my friends about your faith! But what you're doing over here isn't right! It's not who you are, it's not who God is in you. So let's bring it back, get on track, and start moving forward! (Stop sleeping with your parents, Corinthians!)*

His correction wasn't to win the debate or to show everyone how much knowledge he had of the Bible, it was strictly for the purpose of helping other people move forward in life and in a healthier relationship with Christ and each other.

My perception of love is that it speaks up when people are being harmed; it doesn't stay silent while people are being raped and abused by the enemy right in front of you.

Being Wrong Doesn't Equate to Being Stupid

When Hurricane Katrina happened in 2005, I believed it was sent by God and that all of those people had to die because Mardi Gras was full of naked homosexuals dancing around with their "sexually immoral lifestyles."

It makes sense, right? Every Christian knows that God hates homosexuality more than any other sin, and we love to emphasize how much of an abomination it is in His eyes. So to show His unconditional love (but more so His unconditional justice) he wiped out a bunch of men, woman, children and pets (most of whom had nothing to do with the sin that supposedly made Him angry in the first place).

That's totally logical when you're thinking with the mind of a justice-seeking man instead of the mind of a justice seeking God. It's clear that His idea of "justice" is far different than ours in America.

Remember the adulteress caught in adultery? Man's idea of justice in that scenario was for her to be stoned to death, God's idea of justice was, *I don't hold this against you, go and sin no more.*

Who would you rather hang out around?

I was told on the weekend following Katrina that San Francisco was next (as if God has a hit-list and calendar dates) because it too is full of homosexuals. A tidal wave was going to come and take out San Francisco and it would fall into the ocean with a major part of California (fear-mongering "prophets" have been threatening us Californians with that for years!)

The worst part is that I live twenty minutes away from San Francisco, so that tidal wave would have taken me out as well. I remember as soon as I was told that, I prayed silently and said, "God, I don't really understand how that judgment stuff works, but I know you're a just God and you have a good reason for it!"

Translation: "I'm not sure why I have to die because of their sin, but you always have good reasons for everything, right?"

I believed that junk, not because I was stupid or homophobic, but because I didn't know any better—I was ignorant of the Truth about God. I didn't know how to look for Truth on my own, so the best I could do was take it from the people I trusted to spoon feed me (pastors, friends, televangelists, and whoever was in a position of church leadership).

Do I think whoever told me that about Katrina was stupid for believing it? Some of you reading this might, but no, I don't. They didn't know any better, just like I didn't. Just like a preschooler who writes his R's backwards isn't stupid, they just don't know how to write them forward yet. But they learn as they grow, as people correct them and teach them.

When truth came along and I found out that, according to what Jesus did, God isn't judging America (no, not even the homosexual community) for sin, I dropped all of that garbage I had previously believed about my Father and His creation. I started writing my R's the correct way. I knew God personally through Jesus, rather than through the judgmental filter of other Christians.

I didn't feel bad or stupid for having believed those lies for my entire life; instead I celebrated the fact that I had just encountered the Truth—and when you know the Truth, He will set you free.

It's All about Jesus

Most people's measuring rod of Truth isn't Jesus; it's their own preconceived ideas and prejudices towards other people.

Why could I so easily accept that Katrina was sent to warn gay people to stop being gay? Because I had already believed the idea that God didn't like homosexuality. "You can't keep breaking God's laws! He won't put up with it forever! He is a just God!"

Much of Christianity today isn't about knowing Jesus (which is eternal life according to John 17:3). Instead it's about getting your behavior right so you can avoid sin and hell. Christians know more details about rules and Hell than they do about the person of Christ.

We know what we can and can't do and we can spot another person's sin from a mile away. And even though it's clearly forbidden in scripture, there are people who have "been to hell and back" and have written detailed books about the ins-and-outs of it to warn everyone to work as hard as they can to impress God so they don't have to go there (compare to what Jesus said in Luke 16:19-31).

We know what every hallway, every room, and all the picture frames on the walls of hell look like, and yet, we still find ourselves confused about the Person of Christ, and "what would Jesus do?"

Most of the time, the Jesus we preach doesn't even know what the heck He's doing Himself, does He? He's as a double-minded and lukewarm as He told us not to be.

"Do I heal this person or not?"

"Is this a good time for them to lose their mother?"

"Should I send Julie to Africa or India for missions?"

"Should I redirect this catastrophic hurricane to Japan or Mississippi? Which has more sin?"

"Which doors should I open or close in Daniel's life this week?"

What would Jesus do more often becomes a super-spiritual sounding, unbiblical version of *what would I do*? And that's often how we figure out how to treat ourselves and others. Not by how Jesus is in scripture, but by how Jesus is in our presumptions, which are often the result of looking at Him through a lens of fear and judgment, rather than a lens of perfect love (which drives out fear [John 4:18]).

In an attempt to justify ourselves we make things up like, "If I made a bunch of rules, and people kept breaking them, I'd punish them after a while! I showed them kindness and mercy for a little bit, but they just took my kindness for weakness! They can't just walk on me like that. I'm a Christian, not a doormat! They need to be taught a lesson!"

We somehow conclude that those ideas must have come from the Holy Spirit just because they popped into our head, and so that must also be God's perspective on the matter as well. So we start telling other people things like, "God cannot put up with our sin forever! If He doesn't judge America He'll have to apologize to Sodom and Gomorrah!"

We become so self-centered in our pursuit of justice and judgment against the wicked (based on our own opinions of what wickedness is) that we completely forget that the guy who perfectly represented God said "seventy times seven" to the guy looking for any reason to stop forgiving. And that one of the most quoted chapters in Biblical history (the love chapter in 1 Cor. 13) says "love keeps **no record** of wrongs."

We still get behind our pulpits and insist that God is angry and vindictive, and we make Him look like a bad father while we get to look like the heroes jumping in front of Daddy's shotgun whenever He stands up and aims it at America—crying out for mercy as if we want it more than He does.

Do you see why so many non-Christians think Christians are crazy? It's not because we believe in God as much as it's the *kind of God* we believe in.

Speaking Up

It's as if our siblings have been running around for the longest time, telling everybody that our Father is a bipolar psychopath with an itchy trigger finger. The townsfolk are scared out of their minds and want Him removed, yet those of us who actually know Him have been sitting at home, scared to speak up and say, "I know my Father and He's nothing like that!"

We don't want to make our siblings feel bad for having spread a bunch of lies. We don't want to "cause division" or make it look like we aren't united, or any of the other nonsensical excuses we've invented to be irresponsible and compromising towards the things that destroy people's lives. So instead we sit back in apathy while our (probably well-intentioned) siblings spin their own little hurricanes of destruction over the hearts and minds of men regarding our Father.

By the time we do finally go out and say, "My father is so kind, he wants to hang out and be your friend," we're looked at as if we're crazy, and told, "No thank you. I heard about your Father. He's a homophobic bigot who massacres entire cities because gay people live there. He kills people to show His disapproval of people who kill people. Tell him to stay far, far away from us. We want nothing to do with him!"

Then we get in church on Sunday and preach sermons about how rebellious those people are towards God. They really aren't rebelling against God, they're just using common sense based on what the people who claim to know God said about Him. That's their only frame of reference for what God is like, and it's more often than not a terrible one. He sounds like a life-threatening psycho, and who would honestly get excited about hanging out with a life-threatening psycho that might decide to murder you at any second if you do something He doesn't approve of? He's unpredictable and full of rage.

We excuse (and expose) our belief in His split personalities with sayings like, "He is Love, but He is also just!" Listen, I believe He's Love and just, too. But I don't believe there are moments where the just part of Him takes over to such an extent, that it makes Him act unloving towards the very same people He promised to love unconditionally. I don't believe He kills His enemies when it was His Son who gave us the command to "love your enemies."

Love and Justice come from the same Person, *as* the same Person. He doesn't have mood swings. He doesn't get angry and turn into a giant green monster whenever Gentiles refuse to live by a list of ancient Jewish laws.

Where Do We Go From Here?

We want the entire world to know Jesus, and there's nothing wrong with that, but the best place to start is getting to know Him for ourselves. And you can really begin to do that by getting in The Book and studying the life of Jesus for yourself.

Who did He hang around with? Who did He protect? Who did He heal? How did He respond to accusations and threats from religious people? How did He treat governmental authorities?

It's perfectly fine for you to ignore the Old Testament for awhile until you have a better understanding of who God is as seen through the life of Jesus. Ignore those 'read the Bible in 1 year' devotionals that just toss you back in forth between two covenants with the only goal being to get you through the book as fast as possible.

When you read the Old Testament through the lens of the life of Jesus, and understand that God is "the same, yesterday, today, and forever," then reading the Old Testament becomes a fun adventure rather than a confusing endeavor. You no longer have to constantly create super-spiritual excuses for why a loving God was so destructive towards people.

Then you will understand that those people didn't yet have Jesus living in them, so they didn't yet know God (Luke 10:22). Their perception of God was distorted because they were looking at shadows of God through rules and regulations, not at the reality of God that's found in Christ (Col. 2:17).

You can't give what you don't have. If you have no knowledge of the fullness of Christ in you, or the character of your Father, you can't give that knowledge to anybody else. At best you can only repeat somebody else's sermon. And it will never be said with the authenticity and passion that it would, had it been your words from your heart (and it might not even be an accurate sermon you're repeating anyway).

If you have no knowledge of God according to the life of Christ, then when you read verses like, "be imitators of God" (Eph. 5:1) you end up very confused on how you're even supposed to behave. Do you judge and strike down sinners as God apparently did in the Old Testament? Or do you "reconcile the world to God, not holding their sins against them" as Christ did? (2 Cor. 5:19)

Before you let any word or thought sink into your heart and affect what you believe about God (and as a result, how you behave towards people), line all of it up with the person of Jesus—even if you're the one preaching it.

Keep Hebrews 1:3 and Col. 1:15 close to your heart and at the front of your mind (those two verses have helped me tremendously when it comes to staying grounded). Jesus is what the Father looks like *all the time*. If it doesn't look like the Son, it's not the Father.

You Don't Need Anyone Else To Teach You

In practicing the things I've shared in this book, you'll be able to feed yourself healthy food and get yourself out of the misery of constantly chasing your tail. Best of all, you'll no longer have to wait around for somebody else to give you answers, as they make one promise after another, year after year, "this is the time of your breakthrough", and it never comes.

You're as capable of knowing Jesus on your own as any man or woman who has ever went to Bible college for 15 years and has twelve different theology degrees on the wall of their office.

*As for you, the anointing you received from him **remains in you**, and **you do not need anyone to teach you**. But as **his anointing teaches you about all things** and as that anointing is real, not counterfeit—just as it has taught you, **remain in him**.* (1 John 2:27, NIV)

You don't need to chase all the celebrity church leaders around trying to get a double-portion of their anointing before you can go out and rock the world. You have the Anointed One living in you, and His anointing remains in you. The only way you can lose your anointing is if you lose Him (which is impossible because you've become one spirit with Him [1 Cor. 6:17]).

When they saw the courage of Peter and John and realized that they were unschooled, ordinary men, they were astonished and they took note that these men had been with Jesus. (Acts 4:13, NIV)

This is one of my favorite verses in the entire Bible. Did you notice that they were unschooled? They had no degrees or formal religious education, and yet, they changed the entire known world because they decided to speak up on what they knew about the person of Jesus—even confronting those who were far more educated about religious subjects.

Paul, who was a "Pharisee of Pharisees" knew everything there was to know about scripture, yet he went on to say, *I have resolved to know nothing except Christ and Him crucified.* Paul didn't base his qualifications to preach the gospel on his education, but on his personal relationship with Jesus. He knew Him.

That in no way means education is bad, or that you should drop out of seminary. What it means is that your identity is not based on those credentials. You're not a pastor because you have a piece of paper, you're a pastor because you have a God-given passion to look after God's people and guide them in the right direction.

Ever since I was a little kid I always aspired to be a pastor who could talk to people about Jesus and give them hope as a living. Yet, no matter how much I showed an interest in doing that in the churches I attended, I was never treated like I was qualified enough to do It. I wasn't attending Bible College or trying to serve my way to the top of the religious ladder; I just knew I knew Him and I had great things to share about who He is.

Over and over I watched my friends get invited to speak in youth/college groups, and I waited patiently for an invitation of my own, but it never came. Eventually I worked up the nerve to ask, and I was promptly denied.

When I discovered the platform of social media and that there was no ruling authority who could decide whether or not I was qualified enough to preach the good news to people, I found a way to pastor people without those restrictive religious qualifications and requirements.

At the time of this writing I've been doing that for just about three years, and my words have reached and inspired people all around the world, in countries (and islands) I never knew existed.

A piece of paper doesn't make you a pastor any more than making predictions makes you a prophet. You don't need a Master's in Theology to love people. And I'm not against getting an education, but I don't value papers and positions over personal relationship with Jesus. He's what it's all about.

You can add a fancy religious title in front of your Facebook and Twitter name (Pastor, Prophet, Apostle, Bishop, Reverend, or whatever else you want), but it doesn't mean a thing if you don't know Jesus. Fancy religious titles aren't what changes people's lives long-term, He is. If people are only coming to you because you're waving a title in their face to win their approval and impress them, then you are causing them to put more faith in you than they're putting in the person Jesus.

Christianity was never about *what* you know; it has always been about *Who* you know. We know a lot of *what* nowadays, but not a lot of *Who*.

Now is the time to get back to the roots of Christianity which is nothing more and nothing less than simply knowing Jesus. When you are connected to the Vine, every branch will overflow with life and bear the fruit of the Vine effortlessly.

Thank you for taking the time to read this book.

You are welcomed to share any feedback you have, along with any questions this book might have produced. Head over to the Amazon page and leave a review!

If you're interested in reading more from the author, check out

http://www.saintsnotsinners.org

And join the conversation on Facebook at

http://www.facebook.com/saintsnotsinners

27344766R00094

Made in the USA
Lexington, KY
05 November 2013